# Transactional Awareness.

## NOW I'VE GOT YOU . . . IN BUSINESS

J. ALLYN BRADFORD ■ REUBEN GUBERMAN
Transactional Awareness, Inc.          Block Drug Company, Inc.

# Transactional Awareness®

## NOW I'VE GOT YOU . . . IN BUSINESS

**ADDISON-WESLEY PUBLISHING COMPANY**
Reading, Massachusetts
Menlo Park, California
London
Amsterdam
Don Mills, Ontario
Sydney

# Welcome to our dialogue

What you are about to read (and enjoy, we fondly presume) is the result of a particularly successful collaboration. This book resulted from the application of Transactional Awareness* concepts developed by Allyn Bradford. Using those concepts, we were able to work together for over a year in total harmony but by no means in total unison. It is our belief that the strength of the book is derived from the volatility of the ideas that traveled from one author to the other and back again... and grew in the process. Some history...

Allyn Bradford and Reuben Guberman met in the course of business. Allyn, the analyst, was engaged to present a Transactional Awareness workshop for a sales meeting conducted by the Block Drug Co., where Rube was (and is) Sales Promotion Manager. Drawing on a background that included the scripting of some forty motion pictures and plays, Rube suggested a business-drama format to apply to the special needs of the meeting. The concept met with Allyn's full approval, and several meetings later a specific program was completed. It consisted of a series of playlets, each ending in disarray, an analysis by Allyn of the Transactional Awareness approach to correcting the disarray, and another series of playlets illustrating the successful conclusions that could be reached by the application of Transactional Awareness.

That sales meeting was successful, if the response of those attending is a criterion. But more than an approach to a sales meeting had been forged. It was obvious that the same approach could be taken to business situations that arise every day—to situations that involve every person earning a living at one time or another. Further work built on this base, and pointed the way to including Transactional Awareness Workshop Model materials for each of the situations analyzed. The format of the book was established.

*The term "Transactional Awareness" is registered in the U.S. Patent Office by Transactional Awareness, Inc., Cambridge, Mass.

*Now I've Got You, You Son Of A Bitch* (affectionately known in Transactional Analysis as *NIGYSOB*) is a phrase rarely heard in business dialogues, but too often implied—or, as a matter of fact, nonverbally underlined. It's an unproductive way to carry on a dialogue. The important thing is to know when *NIGYSOB* and its peculiarly pervasive camp followers are entering into a dialogue with potentially destructive results. By the same token, it is quite valuable to know when the dialogue is moving along on an Adult transactional level and approaching fruition of the desired result. The book was written to provide pragmatic assistance in applying Transactional Analysis and further, Transactional Awareness, to real-world experiences, situations with which you, the reader, could easily identify. Without at this point getting into the language of TA in depth, let us point out that each separately structured dialogue, while it has direct bearing on the specific situation under study, can be used to extrapolate truths about interpersonal relationships that occur under a wide variety of circumstances. The conflicts and "boners" (crossed transactions, in TA jargon) that we see in each situation can arise just as well in social encounters as in the business situations illustrated.

Assuming just one generality, that transactions between two people most often take place in the form of a dialogue, the relationship between the co-authors of this book was just that—a dialogue. There was challenge, and response and mutual satisfaction. Each dialogue was written as if it were a short play, with an inordinately unhappy ending. It ended either in conflict or in total loss of communication. This was the challenge from the playwright to the analyst, who did his work and returned the original playlet to the writer with TA logic clearly and effectively applied. The playwright then made comment where appropriate and rewrote the play in the light of the analysis, so that it turned out as nearly successfully as possible.

This flow of material between the authors became a sort of dialogue in itself, with all of the facets of TA action and reaction coming into play in the writing process. No doubt you, the perceptive reader, will, as you become familiar with TA insights, be able to see each of us revealing behavior traits and idiosyncracies in the very context of the book.

The dialogues in the book and the workshop models themselves have been tested in actual seminar situations. We have found that their use stimulated a high level of participant involvement, and were delighted to find that those exposed to the material found it challenging and, indeed, amusing. We hope you will, too, and that each of the very real dialogues in the book will spark a moment of "déjà vu," possibly even some wry amusement, plus some ways to revise your own unhappy endings in real life.

Indeed, if you, our reader, find this work entertaining as well as pragmatically useful, we will have completed a very rewarding and useful dialogue.

*Edison, New Jersey*                                                          R. G.
*March 1978*

# Acknowledgments

The Awareness Format at the end of each chapter is derived from the Communications Model originated by Malcolm Shaw and copyrighted by Educational Systems and Designs, Inc. It appears in detail in *Management Models: The Communication Process*, published by ESD, Westport, Conn., copyright 1967.

My first encounter with this model came through a fortuitous meeting with Charles Reach, a staff member of ESD who was attending a TA workshop I was conducting at the time for the American Management Association in Boston. As a result of that meeting, Charlie and I agreed to create a set of workshop materials to teach TA to management, using the Communications Model combined with TA in a new synthesis which we called Transactional Awareness.

The workshop is currently being used successfully in several major corporations. The ideas for the Awareness Format came directly out of that model and I am extremely grateful to ESD for their kind permission to use their model in this publication.

I would also like to thank George Prince of Synectics, Inc., in Cambridge, Mass., for his creative encouragement over the years, which has led both directly and indirectly to the development of this book.

I would like to acknowledge further my gratitude to Bob and Mary Goulding, co-directors of the Western Institute for Group and Family Therapy, whose potent skill introduced me to Transactional Analysis and self-awareness.

Finally to Ruby, my co-author, who is indeed a jewel and could always somehow respond constructively to my worst writing habits with seemingly infinite patience and resourcefulness, I want to say that the writing of this book with you has been nothing but sheer joy.

*Cambridge, Massachusetts*                                                                 J. A. B.
*March 1978*

# A guide to use of the book

We use the term "use" of the book rather than reading or study, since it is intended to stimulate action. Of course, it is intended to be eminently readable, hopefully thoroughly engrossing and delightful. . . but if that is all it is we will have missed our purpose.

You, the reader, should be actively taking part with us in an analysis of the situations as they occur in the book. Using the Awareness Format for each situational dialogue will be a valuable exercise in applying the concepts of TA to actual situations.

The material offered herein lends itself to classroom work and to seminar applications, using the same approach on a group level.

Each situational dialogue is a chapter in the book, structured as follows:

1. Statement of the situation, including subject, initiator, point of view, and result desired.
2. Original dialogue, without Transactional Analysis insight.
3. Analysis of the dialogue in TA terms.
4. Awareness Format applied to the dialogue.
5. Improved dialogue, after TA adjustments.
6. Awareness Format for application to the reader's own situation.

Each subject represents a situation that is commonly faced in the business world each day. They are all interpersonal communications efforts, some between peers, some between client and salesperson, others between various levels of management and employees.

The situation is clearly and concisely stated. Ramifications of the situation as it applies to the particular dialogue will become apparent in the actual words of the participants. The Initiator, while he or she is always the person who caused the interview or conversation to take place, is not always the one whose Point of View we are examining and therefore both the Initiator and the Point of View are identified. The Desired Result is the one for the participant whose Point of View is being examined.

In each of the original dialogues, something at some point goes awry and results in a situation that cannot produce the Desired Result. An attitudinal problem, or loss of attention, or any one of many influences that can turn a dialogue into a war or a game occurs... hidden from the understanding of the participants.

The dialogue failure is then analyzed under the concepts of Transactional Analysis. The influence or comment or attitude that turned the dialogue in a disastrous direction is brought to light and explained. In some instances, there may well be more than one bad turn in the communications road. A clear understanding of the transactional misstep makes it possible to re-present the dialogue in the light of the information revealed by Transactional Analysis in a way that makes the achievement of the Desired Result more likely. It should be clearly understood that in some cases, the Desired Result quite simply *cannot* be accomplished. In that case, the analysis will point the way toward keeping the lines of communication open and cordial for a future effort.

The notes you make in the Awareness Format after you read the original dialogues will make you a participant in the dialogues rather than merely an observer. And comparing your notes with the Improved Dialogues will indicate to you your progress in understanding the practical application of TA.

As you become involved in a dialogue, you may be reminded of some similar situation of your own. If you would like to work through your own situation to a happier conclusion, use the personal Awareness Format supplied at the end of each chapter. Try it, and you've got yourself in business!

# Contents

## SECTION I

## Employment

## SECTION II

# Change in Employment Status

## SECTION III

# Sales

### 10. We Handle the Whole Thing . . .

### 11. Guaranteed Sale, Right?

### 12. Will It Throw Up on My Shoes?

## SECTION IV

# Miscellaneous

### 13. My Kid Has Got These Red Bumps . . .

### 14. I'm Not Trying to Step on Your Toes . . .

# Introduction

Transactional Awareness is a system for creating a communication style that builds on the insights of Transactional Analysis. In this Introduction we shall first look at some of the general principles of Transactional Analysis (TA) and then see how Transactional Awareness makes use of them.

## OVERVIEW OF TRANSACTIONAL ANALYSIS

Transactional Analysis began on the west coast in 1957 as a new form of group therapy created by Eric Berne, M.D. The book by Berne which first caught the public eye was *Games People Play*, published in 1964. A host of other publications followed. An International Tranactional Analysis Institute now regulates training and publishes a journal for the hundreds of TA therapists and teachers throughout the country. Universities offer courses in TA. New books and articles on the subject appear constantly. TA has revolutionized psychology and its impact has spread far and wide.

The history of Transactional Analysis is full of surprises. Having started out as a new form of therapy it then took many new forms in education, management training and interpersonal communication. In each new phase it explodes with an exciting new set of insights. The reason for its impact is found in its simplicity and precision as a system for describing human behavior. The focus of TA, wherever the application, is on the person and how he or she responds to stimuli from other persons. Each exchange which takes place, consisting of a stimulus and the response, is called a transaction.[1] Transactions occur whenever people communicate, with words, tone of voice and gesture.

Transactional Analysis offers a way for people to respond without being coerced in a given situation. To do that with spontaneity and autonomy they must be aware of the dynamics which are in action. The awareness comes from knowledge of the human personality as depicted by three symbolic circles, which represent ego states, or states of mind[2] (Fig. I.1).

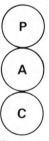

Figure I.1

The circle with the P in it, at the top of this snowman-like figure, is called Parent. It consists of the many teachings from the past by parent figures that are recorded and

1. E. Berne, *Games People Play,* Grove Press, 1964, Chapter 2.
2. D. Jongeward and M. James, *Born to Win,* Addison-Wesley, 1973, Chapter 2.

stored in the brain and which influence behavior in the present. These are like old tape recordings and represent borrowed attitudes, opinions and prejudices. When checked out they may appear to be true or not, on the basis of current evidence.

The checking out is done by the Adult ego state, represented by the middle circle, with the A in it. Adult is sensitive to data in the here and now, dispassionately looking at what is happening, and keeps in direct contact with it.

The Child ego state, represented by the circle with the C, on the bottom, is full of subjective feelings. Some of these are from the past—early life experience—and are "taped in" like the Parent statements. Others arise in response to present stimuli. In the Child are the full range of feelings from joy to despair and also one's intuitive perception of what is happening.

A transaction consists of a stimulus from a given ego state in one person and a response from the same or a different ego state in another. Through TA one becomes aware of which ego state the stimulus is coming from, and to what it is addressed.

For example, the question "What time is it?" can be diagramed as in Fig. I.2.

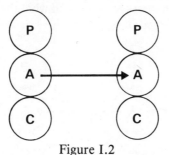

Figure I.2

This will be an example of an Adult-Adult transaction—an exchange of information—if the Adult in the other person responds with that information (Fig. I.3).

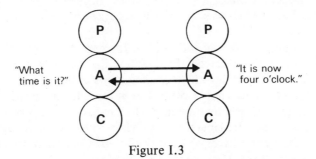

Figure I.3

Such an exchange is called a complementary transaction because the response fits neatly with the stimulus. It comes across as was expected. However, if the other person were to come across with "Why don't you buy a watch!", that is quite different (Fig. I.4).

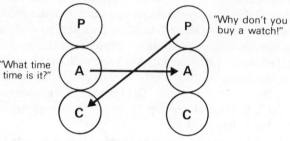

Figure I.4

The latter is called a crossed transaction, and when it occurs communication stops.

A third type of transaction is called ulterior. That occurs when, by tone of voice or gestures, one transmits a message other than what the spoken words convey. For example, consider the transaction begun in Fig. I.5.

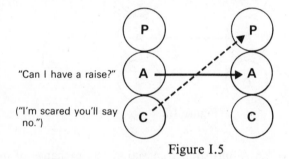

Figure I.5

An ulterior transaction will occur if a person gets influenced by old Parent or Child tapes when talking with his superior about a raise. (The ulterior message is represented by the dotted line.)

It is important to note that the Adult is the part of the personality which can perceive new options and act on them. When the Adult is the executive of the personality it can check out the other ego states, look at the evidence, and then decide what to do. The person need not be controlled by tapes from the past. Since the Adult is results oriented, it is usually the most effective ego state for business situations.

The message transmitted in a transaction is called a stroke. Strokes are verbal or nonverbal, negative or positive. With Adult awareness one has some control over how they are given or obtained. They are so important to our psychological health that any kind at all is better than none. Some people will go for negative ones because they believe that is the only kind available for them. Thus a stroke can be put-down or a word of blame as well as a word of flattery or praise.

Strokes convey a certain personal regard (positive or negative) for someone else and express a basic evaluative attitude. The attitude conveyed in stroking comes from one of four Basic Life Positions.[3]

I'm OK—You're OK.
I'm not-OK—You're OK.
I'm OK—You're not-OK.
I'm not-OK—You're not-OK.

In the first of these, "I'm OK—You're OK," the basic attitude is one of mutual trust. The person giving the stroke trusts and values both himself or herself and the other person. When this occurs, each is more likely to respond appropriately to stimuli from the other.

The second position, "I'm not-OK—You're OK," however, does not allow for constructive action. In this one the person discounts his or her own ability to make a valuable contribution to the transaction. Old Parent tapes tell the Child that he or she cannot do anything right. All he or she can take are negative strokes, which reaffirm this basic "not-OK" belief.

The third Basic Life Position, "I'm OK—You're not-OK," causes a discounting of others. Since they are of no value they must go. The person with that attitude steamrollers other people.

The fourth Basic Life Position is characteristic of the person who is extremely passive. He or she will not take risks and does not believe in anything, and thus is stuck in a quagmire of uncertainty and fear.

The last three of these attitudes come from old tapes in the Parent or the Child which contaminate the Adult with not-OK feelings. When the Adult sorts out these old feelings they can be kept where they belong and not lead to negative judgments about oneself and/or others. The person accepts himself or herself and the other person as personalities of equal worth.

People structure their use of time—and thus the ways they get and give strokes—in six different ways. These are:[4]

Withdrawal
Rituals
Pastimes
Activities
Games
Intimacy

In withdrawal a person is recounting strokes in memory or dreaming of what they might be. Ritual stroking consists of routine or perfunctory exchanges, such as may occur in greeting a person before a conversation begins. A pastime is a diversion that consists of simple complementary transactions, focusing on some subject of mutual

---

3. C. Steiner, *Scripts People Live,* Grove Press, 1974, Chapter 1.
4. E. Berne, *What Do You Say After You Say Hello?,* Grove Press, 1972, Chapter 2.

interest. The participants are not committed to any goal, nor do they look for any big emotional payoff from the conversation. In activities, by contrast, there is commitment to some task performed alone or with others.

A game consists of a series of ulterior transactions which end up predictably in a bad feeling, like being rejected, frustrated or hurt. The game starts with an overt transaction which is seemingly harmless, but it leads into an ongoing series of Parent-to-Child ulterior transactions that end with a put-down of some sort.[5] When analyzed, games look like this:

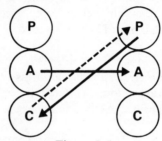

Figure I.6

A common game is *Kick Me*. In *Kick Me* the player receives a kick from the Parent in the other person for some fault or weakness. He or she feels bad but does not know why. The Adult is not aware that the Child is out to collect negative strokes. A person plays this game with someone who is inclined to give out matching strokes. For example, the person who feels ''I'm not-OK—You're OK'' will get it together with someone who feels ''I'm OK—You're not-OK''; the latter plays a game such as *Now I've Got You*, abbreviated *NIGY*. In its hard form *NIGY* becomes *NIGYSOB (Now I've Got You, You Son of a Bitch)*.

Games always end badly and prevent intimacy, because they do not allow for freedom or spontaneity in the other person. Intimacy has an element of risk; and when it occurs all the ego states come into play. Strokes given and received in intimacy are just for what you are, because you're you.

Games are like little scenes in a life script, in which a plot unfolds and a part is played. Depending on the plot, the role consists of Victim, Persecutor or Rescuer. These interact with each other in a drama triangle:[6]

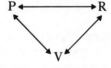

5. J. Meininger, *Success Through Transactional Analysis,* Grosset & Dunlap, 1973, Chapter 5.

6. S. Karpman, ''Script Drama Analysis,'' *Transactional Analysis Bulletin,* 7:26, April 1968, pp. 39-43.

The Persecutor attacks the Victim, and the Rescuer tries to help. After enough bad feelings build up they dramatically change roles—i.e., the Victim attacks either the Persecutor or the Rescuer. The energy moving around the triangle does not lead to problem solving.

A common occurrence that may cause a switch from one role to another in the drama triangle is called "stamp collecting." Much as trading stamps at the supermarket are saved and then cashed in for prizes, "gold" and "brown" psychological trading stamps also may be saved and cashed in for prizes. These psychological trading stamps are good and bad feelings wangled from stroke-getting experiences.

Gold stamps are collected for prizes such as buying oneself an expensive gift, or going on a trip somewhere. The gold stamp collector simply doesn't feel OK enough without the stamps to get out of the Victim role. But with them he or she can play Rescuer, and get prizes.

A dramatic role switch is made by the brown stamp collector when he or she builds up "enough" negative feelings. Then a bad scene in that person's script follows. Five books of stamps may be enough to change that person's role from Victim to Persecutor. Then the boss gets told off, or even a friendly Rescuer may come under attack. The prize is obtained when the brash action occurs.

The stamp collector does not really change anything, since he or she is only playing games. Change will occur only when the Adult is aware of the game and decides to act on an option that will lead to constructive results.

This brief summary recapitulates the major concepts of TA as they are used in this book. Clearly, however, some TA background by the reader is assumed by the authors. If you do not have that, we recommend that you read *Born to Win* by Jongeward and James or *The Practical TA Manager* by Morrisson and O'Hearne to gain a more comprehensive understanding of basic TA concepts.

The purpose of this book is to engage the reader in applying these concepts to everyday business situations, and to do that we take steps into Transactional Awareness.

"Transactional Awareness does with T.A. what Edison did with electricity: it arranges a few basic elements into a new combination that makes power and light," according to Dick Blue, a seasoned trainer who participated in one of the workshops. This new combination of transactional elements that has produced the power and light of dialogues that reach constructive and viable conclusions is described here in detail.

## TRANSACTIONAL AWARENESS

There are four basic ways to communicate:

1. You can tell the other person what to do.
2. You can have the other person tell you what to do.
3. You can get together and mutually agree.
4. You can decide not to do anything.

These four options exhaust the possibilities in any situation. Each of these can be readily identified by the Adult and, by using Transactional Awareness, the most appropriate one can be developed for any situation.

Just as Transactional Analysis shows how the Child once developed games to support a Basic Life Position, Transactional Awareness shows how the Adult can now develop strategies to achieve a Desired Result.

Transactional Analysis shows how the games people play are unconscious patterns of behavior ending in bad feelings, broken relationships or worse. Games originate as strategies to obtain strokes. In the grownup, games are activated by the Child or the Parent.

Transactional Awareness uses the same principles, but it starts from the here-and-now awareness of the Adult in the mature person. In Transactional Awareness, the four Basic Life Positions are transformed into *situational options*, rather than static attitudes toward life. These are diagrammed as follows:[7]

<table>
<tr><td></td><td colspan="2" align="center">U +</td><td></td></tr>
<tr><td rowspan="2">I–</td><td>Get Away<br>From</td><td>Get On<br>With</td><td rowspan="2">I +</td></tr>
<tr><td>Get Nowhere<br>With</td><td>Get Rid<br>OF</td></tr>
<tr><td></td><td colspan="2" align="center">U–</td><td></td></tr>
</table>

Frank Ernst calls this representation the "OK Corral." Here is what the four quadrants mean:

I– U + "Get Away From"—the Child runs away and hides.

I– U– "Get Nowhere With"—the Child is on a trip to Nowheresville.

I + U– "Get Rid Of"—the Child is attacking other people through the Critical Parent.

I + U + "Get On With"—the Adult accepts the Child in oneself and others realistically.

Transactional Awareness looks at all these quadrants from the Adult point of view. Instead of being the basis for a script, they now represent different approaches

7. Frank Ernst, "The O.K. Corral: The Grid for Get-On-With," *Transactional Analysis Journal,* Vol. 1, No. 6 (October 1971).

to dealing with the present situation. These approaches, or styles, can be illustrated graphically as follows.[8]

Relinquishing                                                 Developmental

| Following the lead taken by the other person | Inviting some give and take with the other person |
|---|---|
| Withdrawing from the other person | Providing a structure to be followed by the other person |

Defensive                                                 Controlling

Now suppose we put the Adult circle in the middle of the OK Corral, like this.

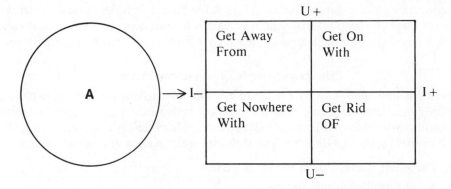

When the Adult circle moves into the OK Corral, all the parts inside that circle are OK.

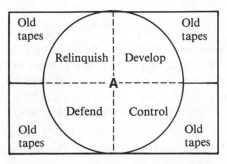

---

8. For further study in this application of Behavioral Science concepts read *Management of Organizational Behavior* by Hersey and Blanchard, published by Prentice-Hall, 1977.

The four quadrants *for the Adult* represent the four options in any situation. The space outside the Adult circle represents old tapes—even Adult tapes that have not been updated. The effectiveness of the option depends on the factors present in a given situation. The Adult can check out these situational factors and then develop an appropriate style to achieve the result desired in that situation.

In any situation the brain is geared to quickly assess and then retrieve a response to whatever stimulus comes along. However, that response will be automatically an "old tape," which may result in ineffective communication, *unless our Adult begins to function*. If we pause to use our Adult, we can then check out the situation further and *decide* how best to respond in that situation, fully aware of the choice we have made. Not only are we more likely to attain our Desired Result when we do that, but we can also *learn* from the results, whatever they are. When our Adult is functioning, we are less concerned about being "right" or "wrong" and more concerned about what the results teach us.

In this book, the Awareness Format which follows the analysis of each dialogue is designed to change old Parent and Child tapes to Adult statements, and to change ulterior transactions, games, and roles into Adult behavior. It shows how to identify each of these blocks to effective communication in your own real life situations and how to develop a communications style which will attain the Desired Result for you.

### Criteria for Selecting Transactional Styles

**Developmental Style.** This style is one of give and take, asking and telling, exploring options together and sharing opinions. It is both active and passive. It gives a cordial reception to the ideas of others and makes a forthright presentation of one's own. Out of it creative ideas can develop. The Developmental style is appropriate when:

1. The Adult is available in the other person.
2. A joint decision is important.
3. An impasse has been reached and a new approach is desired.
4. There is time for study and discussion.

Let us see how these criteria apply in various situations.

1. *The Adult is available in the other person.* When this is true there can be give and take with intelligent and informed opinions. Clark Burley, in the dialogue titled "I can play that paper game" (Chapter 4), assumes this criterion applies but is not aware that he is being influenced by his Child tapes. If he had checked out these tapes, he could have made Adult-Adult contact instead of losing out.

2. *A joint decision is important.* A Developmental style opens the way for the other person to become part of the decision. He or she will then identify with the results and feel a sense of loyalty and commitment.

3. *An impasse has been reached and a new approach is desired.* If you need a breakthrough, the Developmental style considers new alternatives and will help you see the problem in a different light. Developing new alternatives may require holding

back your Parent and giving some free play to your intuition, which comes from your Child.

4. *There is time for study and discussion.* The Developmental style takes time and does not work well under extreme pressure. It is democratic. To some this process may appear to be inefficient because it takes longer.

**Controlling Style.** This style gives direction to the other person. It is usually efficient and task oriented. The development of the other person is not a priority. When used appropriately, it can be highly effective in producing results. The Controlling style is appropriate when:

1. The chief priority is to get the task done as soon as possible.
2. You intend to direct the project in your own way.
3. Ready assent is forthcoming from the other person's Child.
4. Negotiation is futile, and you control all the alternatiaves.

The Controlling style is characterized by telling others what to do. It does not negotiate. The person assumes he or she has the authority, right and power to give directions and that others are uninformed or disoriented.

1. *The chief priority is getting the task done.* In some situations there may be no time to solve problems cooperatively. You may have to take over forcefully and give orders from your Parent.

2. *You intend to direct the project in your own way.* If you assume that you are informed and the others are not, it is not useful to ask for their thoughts or opinions. In the situational dialogue "Despite your lousy environment" (Chapter 3), Rex Primero acts on this assumption, but his Adult has not checked out his Parent tapes, so it ends in disaster.

3. *Ready assent is forthcoming from the other person's Child.* The Controlling style may save time if others are in their Child and *expect* to be told what to do. However, if they are *resistant*, the Controlling style may be self-defeating.

4. *Negotiation is futile and you control all the alternatives.* When you have exhausted the possibilities for rational discussion and something must be done, to give an ultimatum may be appropriate, providing you really do have the power to enforce your decision.

**Relinquishing Style.** This is characterized by careful listening, understanding and encouragement. It leaves the initiative with the other person but loyally comes through when needed. It makes a realistic appraisal of other people and then seeks to develop their potential.

The Relinquishing style is appropriate when:

1. The other person has relevant information which you do not possess.
2. The other person's Child is upset and needs your Nurturing Parent.

3. Development of the other person's autonomy is the most important objective.

4. The other person is autonomous, yet a caring relationship still exists.

1. *The other person has information which you do not possess.* When you are not informed, no matter what your position is in the organizational structure, communication cannot be effective if the other person hears uninformed opinions from you, which are coming from old tapes. When others do have expertise, no matter how large or small, your recognition of it will develop their confidence in themselves and their respect for you.

2. *The other person's Child is upset and needs your Nurturing Parent.* When a person is emotionally upset, whether for job-related or personal reasons, he or she may need you to stay with them through that time, supportively, rather than to get into problem solving or giving directives. Also, it is better to stroke them in a caring way than to try to analyze their problems psychologically. Mary, in "My kid has these red bumps" (Chapter 13), may well be a person who qualifies for a Nurturing Parent treatment rather than the Critical Parent she gets from the branch manager.

3. *Development of the other person's autonomy is the most important objective.* In working with subordinates whom you expect to take responsibility and use initiative in their work, you may need to combine a strategy of Adult-Adult transactions with Parent-Child ones. Timing is important and risks have to be taken—risks which you can afford, when you let the other person make decisions. The personnel manager in "I'm not trying to step on your toes" (Chapter 14) would have done much to boost Larry's morale if he had tuned in to the here and now rather than his old Parent tapes. He probably would have needed to combine a Relinquishing style with a Controlling one but his Adult could have been capable of doing that quite readily, as indicated in the Improved Dialogue. One may shift from one style to another when the requirements of the criteria have been met.

4. *The other person is autonomous yet a caring relationship still exists.* Autonomy occurs when you develop someone successfully by giving him or her more responsibility. Though that person is not dependent on you any more, you still take some pride in what he or she does, and the person still wants some recognition from you. A controlling or even a Developmental style, at this stage, would only get in such a person's way; but you don't want to use a Defensive style because your strokes are still important to him or her.

**Defensive Style.** This may be regarded as negative behavior because it discounts, or withholds strokes. However, there are some situations when that is appropriate. A Defensive style may be adopted with poise and tact, by politely disdaining to be caught up in a situation where one simply does not belong. Acceptable Parent rituals can readily be mustered by the Adult for a gracious retreat.

The Defensive style is appropriate when:

1. Your Child is confused or frustrated.

2. Participation is against the moral standards of your Parent.

3. Your support is not required.

4. You are aware that games are being played.

1. *Your Child is confused or frustrated.* If your Adult is aware of what is going on, then by discounting you can avoid dumping that bad feeling all over the place, like Harry in "I got nothin' against them jigs" (Chapter 9). Retreating from the situation will give you time to cool down so you can check out the tapes and act rationally.

2. *Participation is against the moral standards of your Parent.* If your Adult has checked out these tapes and judges them valid, you clearly have no business being in that situation and should retreat by the most expedient path.

3. *Your support is not required.* Sometimes it is best to completely get out of a situation and adopt a policy of benign neglect. Here you may have to turn off Nurturing Parent tapes that try to be helpful but really only get in the way.

4. *You are aware that games are being played.* Often, spotting a game is enough to bring it to an end. It takes two to play, and if one person stops, the game is over.

When a person chooses a style as a result of checking out a situation, he or she is operating from the Adult. Even so, a person may decide to use one or another ego state to implement that style—that is, he or she may decide to use the Nurturing Parent because the other person's Child is upset. James Courtly does this in the Improved Dialogue for "My kid has these red bumps," Chapter 13, when his Adult turns on his Nurturing Parent and he responds to the needs of a client with a sick child.

It will happen very differently, however, if the behavior does not originate in the Adult. Even Relinquishing behavior can undermine effective communication if it comes from the not-OK Child which is playing games.

Transactional Awareness works effectively when there is sufficient energy in the Adult to respond to a situation in ways that are OK.

## USING THE PRINCIPLES

To help you apply TA principles and gain skill in selecting transactional styles, we have developed a format to achieve Adult awareness in situations of your own as well as those we have presented in this book. The Awareness Format takes you through a step-by-step process similar to the one we use in working with the dialogues. This format was the means by which the dialogues were revised. We hope that you can use the Awareness Format in your own situations in a way that is equally useful. The format is designed to get you out of your old script and to put you in the here-and-now situation, with all your Adult potency available.

An Awareness Format and an Improved Dialogue are provided for each chapter as a model for how to improve a situation of your own. You need not take it literally. Use your own imagination some, and experiment with the format in different ways. Then keep the parts that work best for you.

When you work through a particular situation in the book, such as asking for a pay raise or refusing one, do the parts provided to develop a new transactional style. Then check our Improved Dialogue against your own ideas. Finally, use both sets of ideas—yours and ours—as a model of how to work through problems of your own.

By using the Awareness Format in this way, we hope you will be able not only to rewrite the dialogues in this book but to become the author of creative dialogues in your own life situation.

# SECTION ONE
# Employment

# CHAPTER ONE

# If only they had paid attention to my memos . . .

**Subject:** Applying for executive employment
**Initiator:** Applicant
**Point of View:** Applicant
**Desired Result:** To get the job
**Applicant:** Sam Goodwork     **Interviewer:** Harry Dubious

Sam Goodwork strides into Dubious's office, his hand extended in greeting. Dubious has risen from behind his desk, has his hand extended. As they shake hands over the desk:

**Sam:** My name is Sam Goodwork, Mr. Dubious, and I appreciate this opportunity.

**Harry:** Nice to see you. Please, sit down.

Sam is seated facing Dubious across the desk. Dubious is obviously taking a moment to refamiliarize himself with Sam's application, which is before him. As he shuffles the papers, Sam speaks.

**Sam:** You'll find that my experience fits right into your operation, Mr. Dubious. I've managed some of the biggest discount stores in the business. Matter of fact, I'm proud to say that in my career, there isn't an aspect of the operation that I haven't directly handled. I took the trouble to check out a few of your stores before I came up, and I can tell you, Mr. Dubious, that I could...

**Harry:** (*Rather matter of factly*) We'll get to all that, Goodwork. I notice that you were making $22,500 at your last job. Our scale starts below that, you know. Are you prepared to accept less money?

**Sam:** Well... how much less?

**Harry:** I thought you were aware of the pay offered before you applied. In any case, the job pays $18,500.

**Sam:** Oh, sure, I knew what the stated scale was, but you know how those things are. I thought I'd sort of get it straight from you...(*Laugh*)

**Harry:** You got it straight. Is it acceptable?

**Sam:** Well... sure. I'm sure that a man has a chance to prove himself and move up financially...

**Harry:** We have a store manager's incentive program that you'll be eligible for, if you come with us, in a year. You're familiar with the regular fringe benefits, I assume?

**Sam:** Oh, yes, I am, and they're totally satisfactory.

**Harry:** Fine. Now, if you don't mind, I'd like you to tell me briefly exactly what responsibilities you had when you managed the Duper Discount.

**Sam:** As you know, Mr. Dubious, they went bankrupt, which is why I'm available...(*Laugh*) but I can tell you that the store I managed made a profit! Why, if only they had paid attention to the memos that I kept sending to the guys upstairs, I bet they wouldn't have gone bankrupt! Could you believe that they had a system where the senior buyers didn't have to...

**Harry:** Excuse me, Mr. Goodwork, I'm sure that's quite interesting, but could you be more specific about your duties? Did you do all the hiring and firing for the store? Any contact with EEOC? How personally did you get involved in display?... that sort of thing.

**Sam:** Did I have any contact with EEOC? Better believe it, I did! They tried to shove people down my throat... Well, I don't have to tell you in your position what a problem it is. I got along OK though... We never lost a single case.

**Harry:** You had several?

**Sam:** Well, actually, only two in the four years I was there. The fact is I didn't directly do the hiring and firing, that was handled by department managers... with my approval or disapproval, of course. I just wanted to emphasize to you that I know what the EEOC is and how to work around, that is, within, their rules.

**Harry:** Mr. Goodwork, thank you very much for coming in. As soon as we've made a decision, I'll call you personally. (*Rises and sticks out hand.*)

**Sam:** Oh yeah, sure... but I think you ought to know how I got volume in my store up to twice what it was when I took over, and we won several display awards and I hope you got a chance to look at the commendation letters in my file... I mean...

**Harry:** You have a very impressive background, Mr. Goodwork, and I thank you for coming in. Goodbye. You'll surely hear from us.

### ANALYSIS: PARENTAL PERMISSION TO SUCCEED
#### Applying for Executive Employment

**Script Theme**: "You never thought I was good enough."
**Tapes:** Parent—"Make a good impression, Son."
　　　Child—"I'm scared your standards are too high."
**Key Crossed Transaction:**

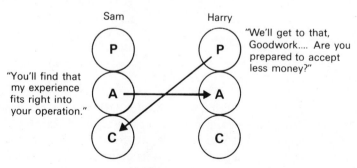

Figure 1.1

**Ulterior Message:** "Tell me I don't qualify."

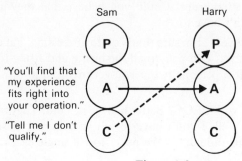

Figure 1.2

**Basic Life Position:** "I'm not-OK—you're OK."
**Games:** *Ain't it Awful, Kick Me*
**Role:** Victim ("They went bankrupt, which is why I'm available.")

The dialogue which controls the outcome is not between Sam and Harry. It is between Sam's Child ego state and his Parent ego state. For whatever reasons, Sam's Parent tapes do not give him permission to be a genuine success. So he just plays at it instead.

He starts by trying to make a good impression. But his Adult does not tune in on the specific information Harry wants. Nor does it tune in on Harry's heavy Parent, which is going to be very demanding in the interview. He ends up overstating himself and unloading a lot of irrelevant data. He finds himself once again put down by his Parent tape, and the put-down is reinforced by Harry's Parent. That negative stroke reaffirms his basic life position: "I'm not-OK—You're OK."

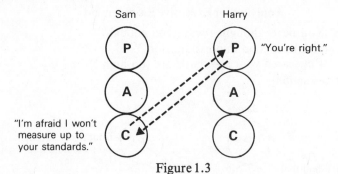

Figure 1.3

It is one more scene in Sam's script, which has for its theme, "You never thought I was good enough." Evidently he did not get enough strokes from his parents for doing well as a young child, but was only blamed for doing poorly. Now he puts Daddy's face on other authority figures. So his script acts as a negative stroke collector. By using his Adult instead of his not-OK Child, he could have slipped out of his script. But that may have seemed too risky and so he preferred to stay in his role of Victim, where all the lines to be spoken were familiar.

His games emerge as the climax of the plot, with his Parent saying "Ain't it awful" and his Child saying "Kick me." His Parent tends to blame others: "Why, if only they had paid attention to the memos that I kept sending to the guys upstairs, I bet they wouldn't have gone bankrupt!" It does not respond to the here-and-now stimulus from Harry's Adult, which is a request for specific information about his previous duties as store manager. His Parent is vaguely generalizing about the irresponsible behavior of others, without making Sam take any responsibility himself for what happened.

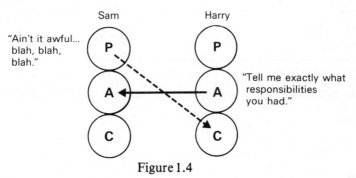

Figure 1.4

The result of all this is that Sam's Child gets "kicked" when he tries to come up with the data that is asked for. It is already too late. His stuffy and devious Parent has already sent the message to Harry that here is a person who does not communicate well and who is not trustworthy. Sam's Child feels rejected and wonders why. If his Adult were aware of the feeling and could check out how it happened, Sam could then consider what other options there are to take in his next interview. If his Adult does not process that information, his make-believe script will seem like reality. How would you rewrite this dialogue if you were the author?

---

## Awareness Format

Revise the script by writing your own version of this dialogue, which has ended so badly. Use the Awareness Format to do it, and then compare your version with ours. A sample for the Awareness Format is provided in the appendix.

### I. Tapes

Change Sam's Child tape ("I'm scared your standards are too high.") into an Adult statement.

Adult: _____

---

Change Sam's Parent tape ("Make a good impression, Son.") into an Adult statement.

Adult: _____

_____

## II. Key Crossed Transaction

Change the crossed transaction (see Fig. 1.1) to make it complementary.

Sam: _____

_____

_____

Harry: _____

_____

## III. Ulterior Message

Change Sam's Ulterior Message ("Tell me I don't qualify.") into an Adult statement.

Adult: _____

_____

## IV. Role

Change what Sam said in his Victim role to an Adult statement.

Victim: They went bankrupt, which is why I'm available."

Adult: _____

_____

## V. Style

On a scale from 1 to 10 grade the applicability of each criterion from Sam's point of view. (See the introduction to this book for a detailed explanation of the criteria.)

Grade
1 to 10

A. A Developmental style may be effective:

   1. The Adult is available in the other person.         _____

   2. A joint decision is important.         _____

   3. An impasse has been reached and a new approach is desired.         _____

   4. There is time for study and discussion.         _____

B. A Controlling style may be effective:

   1. The chief priority is to get the task done as soon as possible.         _____

2. You intend to direct the project in your own way. _____

3. Ready assent is forthcoming from the other person's Child. _____

4. Negotiation is futile, and you control all the alternatives. _____

C. A Relinquishing style may be effective:

1. The other person has relevant information which you do not possess. _____

2. The other person's Child is upset and needs your Nurturing Parent. _____

3. Development of the other person's autonomy is the most important objective. _____

4. The other person is autonomous, yet a caring relationship still exists. _____

D. A Defensive Style may be effective:

1. Your Child is confused or frustrated. _____

2. Participation is against the moral standards of your Parent. _____

3. Your support is not required. _____

4. You are aware that games are being played. _____

Fill in the criteria score chart below according to the numbers indicated for each style. Use the criteria score chart to select a transactional style which is designed to effectively achieve Sam's Desired Result.

### Criteria Score Chart

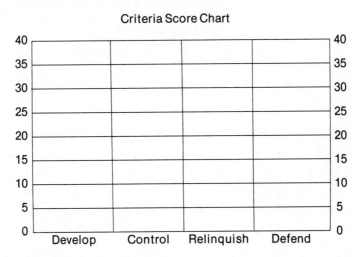

If another style is graded close to the highest one on your chart, you may want to incorporate that in your approach. Both may be appropriate at different times in the dialogue or discussion.

*Strategy*

1. What style is indicated for the Improved Dialogue? _____

_____

2. Make some notes on how Sam's strategy might be improved, using the style indicated.

_____

_____

_____

_____

_____

_____

_____

_____

_____

_____

_____

Now read the Improved Dialogue and compare it with what you have written in Sections I through V.

## THE IMPROVED DIALOGUE
### Applying for Executive Employment

Sam Goodwork strides into Dubious's office, his hand extended in greeting. Dubious has risen from behind his desk, has his hand extended. As they shake hands over the desk:

**Sam:** My name is Sam Goodwork, Mr. Dubious, and I appreciate this opportunity.

**Harry:** Nice to see you, please sit down.

Sam is seated facing Dubious across the desk. Dubious is obviously taking a moment to refamiliarize himself with Sam's application, which is before him.

**Sam:** I'm pretty sure you'll find the background information about my experience fairly complete in the application, Mr. Dubious, but I'd be delighted to fill in any blanks...

**Harry:** (*Matter of factly*) Yes, well, I will have a few questions, but before we get to that, Goodwork, I notice that you were making $22,500 at your last job. Our scale starts below that, you know. Are you prepared to accept less money?

**Sam:** I was aware of the scale before I applied and I came here prepared to accept it... if I'm acceptable to you, and with the understanding that I can improve my financial picture through my own efforts on the job.

**Harry:** That's fair enough. We do have a store manager's incentive program that you'll be eligible for in a year, if you come with us. You're familiar with the regular fringe benefits, I assume?

**Sam:** Yes I am, and they're totally satisfactory.

**Harry:** Fine. Now, if you don't mind, I'd like you to tell me briefly exactly what responsibilities you had when you managed Duper Discount.

**Sam:** To sum it up, I had full responsibility for my store. I did the middle management hiring and firing—department heads and buyers. We did our own buying for the individual stores from an approved list with some leeway... and I kept a veto over the clerks that those people hired. Store layout and display was based on a general planogram, but I supervised the department heads in their individual display decisions.

**Harry:** Have you had any experience with EEOC?

**Sam:** Yes, on two occasions only. We won both cases. The department managers had valid reasons for not hiring the individuals involved and I backed them up. The fact is, we later hired competent minority people for the same jobs.

**Harry:** The Duper Discount company went bankrupt, which of course is why you're available. Quite frankly, did the operation of your store contribute to that bankruptcy?

**Sam:** I can't say flatly yes or no. I wasn't in on the capital investment setup, and I wasn't consulted or informed about the real estate situation. I can say this—my store showed an operating profit each year I was there and, as a matter of fact, volume was doubled during the period of my management. Just to sort of speak out of a sense of pride for a moment, we won several display awards in that store.

**Harry:** Yes. I've seen the commendation letters attached to your resume. Sam, I'd like you to start first thing next week. I've got a store in West Orange that has some problems and I think you're the man to get it on the right track. Let's go over to the accounting office and get some papers filled out...

## Awareness Format Applied to Your Own Situation

### I. Background
Describe briefly a situation in which you have had a responsible part and are not satisfied with the results:

_____

_____

_____

### II. Desired Result
What was your Desired Result? _____

_____

### III. Key Crossed Transaction
In that situation identify a key crossed transaction in which the response came from the Parent or the Child in the other person.

What you said: _____

_____

The response: _____

_____

Diagram your crossed transaction:

### IV. Tapes
Imagine yourself as you were when you were a very young child and think of an experience which is similar to the one you have just described. Be aware of the people who appear in your mind's eye, what you felt and what you were trying to say to them.

In the recent situation which you have just described, what appears to be the Child tape influencing your behavior from that old scene in your past?

Child tape: _____

_____

Change your Child tape into an Adult statement:

Adult: _____

_____

What appears to be your Parent tape? If you need to, go back to the memory you just retrieved for an awareness of that tape.

Parent tape: _____

_____

Change your Parent tape into an Adult statement:

Adult: _____

_____

## V. Ulterior Message

What Ulterior Message did you send to the other person? You can spot your Ulterior Message by examining your Parent and Child tapes to see how they exerted a negative influence on your transactional style in that situation.

Your Ulterior Message: _____

_____

## VI. Basic Life Position

Check out your feelings in that situation. What Basic Life Position do they seem to indicate?

Check one: ☐ I'm not-OK—you're OK.
    ☐ I'm not-OK—you're not-OK.
    ☐ I'm OK—you're not-OK.
    ☐ I'm OK—you're OK.

What is the feeling? _____

## VII. Game Awareness

Now you can see how the parts of your game fall into place. Write here your Desired Result (see II above).

_____

Write here your Ulterior Message (see V above).

_____

Write here the response you got in the crossed transaction (see III above).

_____

Write here your Basic Life Position in that situation (see VI above) and the feeling that goes with it.

Basic Life Position: _____

Feeling: _____

What game seems to be indicated here?

Name: _____

To get out of that game, change your Ulterior Message in that game into an Adult statement.

Adult: _____

_____

## VIII. Role

What role were you playing in that game? Check one:

☐ Persecutor   ☐ Victim   ☐ Rescuer

Describe what you said or did to play that role.

_____

_____

Change that to an Adult behavior or statement:

Adult: _____

_____

## IX. Style

On a scale from 1 to 10 grade the applicability of each criterion from your point of view. (See the introduction to this book for a detailed explanation of the criteria.)

Grade
1 to 10

A. A Developmental style may be effective:

   1. The Adult is available in the other person. _____

   2. A joint decision is important. _____

   3. An impasse has been reached and a new approach is desired. _____

   4. There is time for study and discussion. _____

B. A Controlling style may be effective:

   1. The chief priority is to get the task done as soon as possible. _____

   2. You intend to direct the project in your own way. _____

   3. Ready assent is forthcoming from the other person's Child. _____

   4. Negotiation is futile, and you control all the alternatives. _____

C. A Relinquishing style may be effective:

   1. The other person has relevant information which you do not possess. _____

   2. The other person's Child is upset and needs your Nurturing Parent. _____

   3. Development of the other person's autonomy is the most important objective. _____

   4. The other person is autonomous, yet a caring relationship still exists. _____

D. A Defensive style may be effective:

   1. Your Child is confused or frustrated. _____

   2. Participation is against the moral standards of your Parent. _____

   3. Your support is not required. _____

   4. You are aware that games are being played. _____

Fill in the criteria score chart below, Use the criteria score chart to develop a transactional strategy that will effectively attain your Desired Result.

Criteria Score Chart

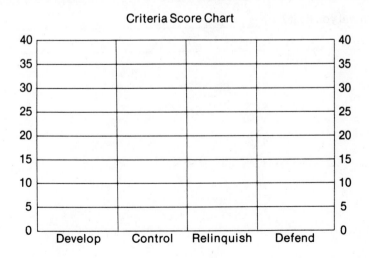

If some other style appears to be close to another one on your chart, you may want to incorporate that in your approach. Both may be appropriate at different times in the dialogue or discussion.

*Strategy*

1. What style is indicated for your Improved Dialogue?

_____

2. Look over carefully what you have written in Sections I-IX and use it to help yourself decide how to implement that style. Then make some notes on what you will do:

_____

_____

_____

_____

_____

_____

_____

_____

_____

3. When will you do it?  _____

_____

# CHAPTER TWO

# We look for a certain approach...

**Subject:** Interviewing prospective executive employee
**Initiator:** Applicant
**Point of View:** Interviewer
**Desired Result:** To obtain enough information about the applicant to
              make a logical judgment
**Applicant:** Harvey Potential      **Interviewer:** Randolph Quiz

Mr. Potential has made application for employment as a sales manager. Basic information about his work history and personal background are already in the hands of Mr. Quiz. That information, provided by Potential in his initial mail job solicitation, has been considered favorable enough to warrant an in-depth interview with the objective of assessing Potential's attitudes and work habits.

Randolph Quiz meets Potential at the door of his office and extends his hand.

**Quiz:** Good afternoon, Mr. Potential. My name is Quiz, Randolph Quiz... won't you sit down?

Quiz leads Potential to a seat opposite his desk, his arm gently over Potential's shoulder guiding him to the seat.

**Potential:** Thank you. Matter of fact, thank you for setting up this interview so promptly. I appreciate it.

**Quiz:** Well, Mr. Potential... mind if I call you Harvey?

**Potential:** Just Harve, that's what I answer to the quickest.

**Quiz:** Fine, Harve, I'm Randy. Listen, it's just the way we do things around here. When I figured that we had a basis for talking together, I had my secretary call you right away. I guess it's working with young people that makes a man act without shilly-shallying, a bunch of boys won't stand around waiting for a leader to make a decision!

**Potential:** Say, I'll bet you're involved with the Boy Scouts... troop leader?

**Quiz:** Matter of fact, yes. Oh, I'm on the Council... the whole volunteer thing, you know. I'm one of those guys that went the whole route... Eagle Scout, more Award Badges than I could count... did me a lot of good. Now, I try to carry on the—well, darn it, the tradition!

**Potential:** Tell the truth, I never had the opportunity to do much scouting... but I can tell you, I've got two sons who are making up for lost time!

**Quiz:** Say, that's fine... (*Suddenly realizing that this is a business conference*) oh... (*Laugh*) we'll have to spend some time talking about scouting some time. For right now, I guess you're here for pretty practical reasons—to talk about the sales manager's job we have open.

**Potential:** Right. I'm sure you've read my resume, so you know I've got the credentials for the job. Well, since I'm familiar with the starting pay package and it's OK with me, I guess the next step is to close the deal... right?

**Quiz:** You surely have the initiative the job needs, Potential. But this isn't a hard-sell situation. We look for a certain approach to the handling of our sales force in this company.

**Potential:** Of course, of course, Mr. Quiz. I can tell you this, I'm a flexible guy. I am perfectly capable of adjusting to corporate policy.

**Quiz:** Say, I wasn't trying to sound officious, there, Harve. I'm sure you can work under our guidelines. Let me get specific. What do you look for in recruiting salesmen? Just a brief outline of your thinking...

**Potential:** Well, Rand... uh, Mr. Quiz... I guess some of those characteristics you found necessary in leading Boy Scouts.

**Quiz:** Frankly, I think we ought to get off the scouting thing and stick to the business world.

**Potential:** Oh,... I just... sure. I look for a guy with gumption, an honest record and the willingness to work hard to better himself. A hungry guy... and if I can add a good track record to that, fine!

**Quiz:** I see. And what about familiarity with our business?

**Potential:** Important, but frankly that's the easiest part to teach.

**Quiz:** Our business isn't that simple, Potential. And you'd find that out pretty quick if you came to work with us!

**Potential:** OK, OK, I'm not putting down the value of knowing this business and the classes of trade and so forth. I honestly feel that a good man can be taught those facts in less time than it takes to teach him to communicate and sell. But if, when I take over, I find that experience in this line is essential, be sure that's what I'll get. I've been in management long enough to make that kind of judgment... and that would be one of the things you'd be paying me for.

**Quiz:** Fine, but there's no need to practice your selling techniques on me, Potential. (*Laugh*) I'm interested only in the facts.

**Potential:** Great. What else do you want to know? And when we're done with talking about my background, there are a few things in that compensation package that need to be cleared up...

## ANALYSIS: A WORLD WHERE THINGS ARE BLACK AND WHITE
### Interviewing Prospective Executive Employee
**Script Theme:** "They don't make 'em like they used to."
**Parent Tapes:** Parent—"You can't trust outsiders."
Child —"Other people have magic powers."

**Key Crossed Transactions:**

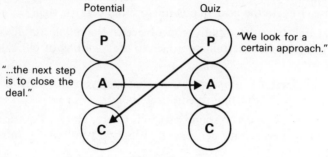

Figure 2.1

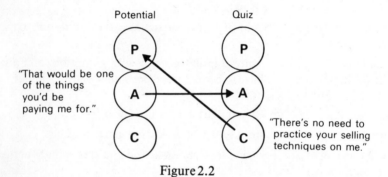

Figure 2.2

**Ulterior Message:** "You do not have it."

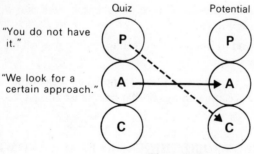

Figure 2.3

**Basic Life Position:** "I'm OK—you're not-OK."

**Game:** *NIGY*

**Role:** Persecutor ("You'd find that out pretty quick if you came to work with us.")

Randy Quiz has a big Parent. He is used to getting strokes for a "job well done." His interest in scouting provides him with "gold stamps" which he collects as good feelings to qualify him for a high position in life and to be better than others. Usually his Parent is the executive of his personality, but occasionally his Child perks up and with wonder in his eyes regards others as having an immense potency (like his parents of long ago) for good or ill, which is unrealistic. When things get too scary he retreats to the protective security of the Parent which will maintain certain traditions (like scouting or company policy) despite whatever spooky things might be lurking around. Safe in the castle of tradition, his Child can be protected by the Parent shooting over the wall at the dragons out there.

In the interview he maintains that he is talking business, but it is the image of scouting which more clearly defines the dynamic. Randy Quiz likes a world in which things are black and white, good and bad, correct and incorrect. And if they aren't one they've got to be the other. Harve may seem willing to adjust, but if he isn't right the first time, he's wrong, and to be wrong is morally unacceptable.

The same response is generated when Randy Quiz sees Harve Potential as being a bit too sharp and slick in the wily ways of making a sale. In this instance what is being sold is Harve himself, but Randy is not buying. He counters Harve's high pressure with his Parent, saying with pious aloofness "we look for a certain approach..." In back of that is a conviction that Harve does not have this approach; but that is not explicitly stated. Though Harve is willing to comply, even eager, that does not count. Randy covers his poisoned apple with sugar coating. Though he secretly knows that Harve will give the wrong answer, he says "I wasn't trying to sound officious..."; and though he says "Let me get specific" he does not mean that. He asks for information from Harve instead, with which he will soon find fault.

Sure enough, Harve slips and slides through his response, trying to second-guess what Randy wants, and finally founders on not including "familiarity with our business" as a key part of what to look for in recruiting salesmen. The question of how they *could* be familiar with it if they were just being recruited is not dealt with. Randy just doesn't want someone smarter than him around who might be more interested in techniques than in the wisdom that comes from long years of association with the company. He doesn't feel you can trust people who don't know where the dog died. His interview with Harve reaffirms his negative judgment about those slick types who haven't got the right facts—or was it the facts right? In Randy's mind it's all the same: "If you're not one of us, you're not-OK."

Randy may sometimes try to rescue people like Harve, by helping to set them straight. But when he does, he ends up the Victim because he is out of his familiar role and that only tends to reaffirm his basic life position, "I'm OK—you're not-OK," which is what he means when he says "Look how hard I tried to help him!"

It is as though Randy had a sign on his desk saying "We look for a certain approach" in front; but on the back it says "but you do not have this approach."

If you were to have all this information in your Adult and you were Randy, how would you rewrite the dialogue?

## Awareness Format

Revise the script by writing your own version of this dialogue, which has ended so badly. Use the Awareness Format to do it, and then compare your version with ours. A sample for the Awareness Format is provided in the appendix.

### I. Tapes
Change Randy's Child tape ("Other people have magic powers.") into an Adult statement.

Adult: _____

_____

Change Randy's Parent tape ("You can't trust outsiders.") into an Adult statement.

Adult: _____

_____

### II. Key Crossed Transactions
Change the crossed transactions (see Figs. 2.1 and 2.2) to make them complementary.

Randy: _____

_____

Harve: _____

_____

Randy: _____

_____

Harve: _____

_____

### III. Ulterior Message
Change Randy's Ulterior Message ("You do not have it.") into an Adult statement.
Adult: _____

_____

### IV. Role
Change what Randy said in his Persecutor role to an Adult statement.
Persecutor: "You'd find that out pretty quick if you came to work with us."

Adult: _____

_____

## V. Style

On a scale from 1 to 10 grade the applicability of each criterion from Randy's point of view. (See the introduction to this book for a detailed explanation of the criteria.)

Grade
1 to 10

A. A Developmental style may be effective:

   1. The Adult is available in the other person. _____

   2. A joint decision is important. _____

   3. An impasse has been reached and a new approach is desired. _____

   4. There is time for study and discussion. _____

B. A Controlling style may be effective:

   1. The chief priority is to get the task done as soon as possible. _____

   2. You intend to direct the project in your own way. _____

   3. Ready assent is forthcoming from the other person's Child. _____

   4. Negotiation is futile, and you control all the alternatives. _____

C. A Relinquishing style may be effective:

   1. The other person has relevant information which you do not possess. _____

   2. The other person's Child is upset and needs your Nurturing Parent. _____

   3. Development of the other person's autonomy is the most important objective. _____

   4. The other person is autonomous, yet a caring relationship still exists. _____

D. A Defensive style may be effective:

   1. Your Child is confused or frustrated. _____

   2. Participation is against the moral standards of your Parent. _____

   3. Your support is not required. _____

   4. You are aware that games are being played. _____

Fill in the criteria score chart below. Use the criteria score chart to develop a transactional strategy that will effectively attain your Desired Result.

Criteria Score Chart

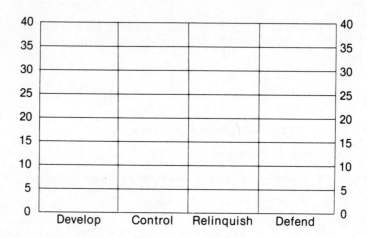

If another style is graded close to the highest one on your chart, you may want to incorporate that in your approach. Both may be appropriate at different times in the dialogue or discussion.

*Strategy*

1. What style is indicated for the Improved Dialogue?  _____

_____

2. Make some notes on how Randy's strategy might be improved, using the style indicated.

_____

_____

_____

_____

_____

_____

_____

_____

_____

_____

_____

_____

Now read the Improved Dialogue and compare it with what you have written in Sections I through V.

## THE IMPROVED DIALOGUE
### Interviewing Prospective Executive Employee

Randolph Quiz meets Potential at the door of his office and extends his hand.

**Quiz:** Good afternoon, Mr. Potential. My name is Quiz, Randolph Quiz... won't you sit down?

**Potential:** Thank you. Matter of fact, thank you for setting up this interview so promptly, I appreciate it.

Quiz starts to put his arm over Potential's shoulder, instead touches his shoulder and points to a comfortable seat opposite his desk. Potential is seated.

**Quiz:** Well, Mr. Potential... mind if I call you Harvey?

**Potential:** Just Harve, that's what I answer to the quickest.

**Quiz:** Fine, Harve. I'm Randy. Listen, it's just the way... I mean I felt we had a basis for talking together so I had my secretary call you right away. I guess it's working with young people that makes a man act without shilly-shallying, a bunch of boys won't stand around waiting for a leader to make a decision!

**Potential:** Say, I'll bet you're involved with the Boy Scouts... troop leader?

**Quiz:** Yes... and more. I've gone the whole route and I take it pretty seriously. Did me a lot of good... and now I sort of try to carry on the—well, darn it, the tradition!

**Potential:** Tell the truth, I never had the opportunity to do much scouting... but I can tell you I've got two sons who are making up for lost time!

**Quiz:** Fine—and we ought to talk more about that some time. For now, I imagine you'd like to get down to the business of that sales manager's job.

**Potential:** Right. I'm sure you've read my resume, so you know I've got the credentials for the job. Well, since I'm familiar with the starting pay package and it's OK with me, I guess the next step is to close the deal... right?

**Quiz:** You surely have the initiative the job needs, Harvey. But this isn't a hard-sell situation. I think you'll agree that we want to find out if you'll be comfortable with the approach the company likes to take to customer relations... and if we'll be comfortable with your way of working.

**Potential:** Fair enough. I'm a flexible guy and I can adjust to company policy.

**Quiz:** Good enough. And you'll find that the company isn't inflexible either. Let me ask some specific questions. What do you look for in recruiting salesmen? Just a brief outline of your thinking...

**Potential:** Well, Randy, I guess some of those characteristics you'd find in the scouting world...

**Quiz:** I have no argument with the aims of scouting, obviously... But I'd prefer a more specific relationship to selling and business...

**Potential:** Good enough. I look for a guy with gumption, and an honest record and the willingness to work to better himself. A hungry guy, and if I can add a good track record to that—fine!

**Quiz:** I see. Do you place any emphasis on familiarity with our business?

**Potential:** Sure, but not as much as the general qualifications I talked about. Business jargon and details are the easiest things to teach.

**Quiz:** I think perhaps you feel that way now because you're not totally familiar with the complexities of our operation...

**Potential:** That's possible. I would never put down the value of knowing the classes of trade and merchandise facts and so on... and if as I get into the job I find that training time should be oriented more heavily in that direction, I'll certainly do that. My track record will prove that I can set up the right kind of program for an existing business problem. As a matter of fact, that's the kind of judgment you'd be paying me for.

**Quiz:** Fine, but there's no need to—that is, I think I've seen a solid example just now of your own selling technique. I'm impressed... but why don't you relax and assume we can work out the details of your coming with us so that we can talk over some of the real problems you'll face in that sales manager's job.

**Potential:** Fair enough.

## Awareness Format Applied to Your Own Situation

### I. Background
Describe briefly a situation in which you have had a responsible part and are not satisfied with the results:

_____

_____

_____

### II. Desired Result
What was your Desired Result? _____

_____

### III. Key Crossed Transaction
In that situation identify a key crossed transaction in which the response came from the Parent or the Child in the other person.

What you said: _____

_____

The response: _____

_____

Diagram your crossed transaction:

### IV. Tapes
Imagine yourself as you were when you were a very young child and think of an experience which is similar to the one you have just described. Be aware of the people who appear in your mind's eye, what you felt and what you were trying to say to them.

In the recent situation which you have just described, what appears to be the Child tape influencing your behavior from that old scene in your past?

Child tape: _____

_____

Change your Child tape into an Adult statement:

Adult: _____

_____

What appears to be your Parent tape? If you need to, go back to the memory you just retrieved for an awareness of that tape.

Parent tape: _____

_____

Change your Par, it tape into an Adult statement:

Adult: _____

_____

## V. Ulterior Message
What Ulterior Message did you send to the other person? You can spot your Ulterior Message by examining your Parent and Child tapes to see how they exerted a negative influence on your transactional style in that situation.

Your Ulterior Message: _____

_____

## VI. Basic Life Position
Check out your feelings in that situation. What Basic Life Position do they seem to indicate?

Check one:  ☐ I'm not-OK—you're OK.
            ☐ I'm not-OK—you're not-OK.
            ☐ I'm OK—you're not-OK.
            ☐ I'm OK—you're OK.

What is the feeling? _____

## VII. Game Awareness
Now you can see how the parts of your game fall into place. Write here your Desired Result (see II above).

_____

Write here your Ulterior Message (see V above).

_____

Write here the response you got in the crossed transaction (see III above).

_____

Write here your Basic Life Position in that situation (see VI above) and the feeling that goes with it.

Basic Life Position: _____

Feeling: _____

What game seems to be indicated here?

Name: _____

To get out of that game, change your Ulterior Message in that game into an Adult statement.

Adult: _____

_____

## VIII. Role

What role were you playing in that game? Check one:

☐ Persecutor    ☐ Victim    ☐ Rescuer

Describe what you said or did to play that role.

_____

_____

Change that to an Adult behavior or statement:

Adult: _____

_____

## IX. Style

On a scale from 1 to 10 grade the applicability of each criterion from your point of view. (See the introduction to this book for a detailed explanation of the criteria.)

Grade
1 to 10

A. A Developmental style may be effective:

    1. The Adult is available in the other person.    _____

    2. A joint decision is important.    _____

    3. An impasse has been reached and a new approach is desired.    _____

    4. There is time for study and discussion.    _____

B. A Controlling style may be effective:

   1. The chief priority is to get the task done as soon as possible. _____

   2. You intend to direct the project in your own way. _____

   3. Ready assent is forthcoming from the other person's Child. _____

   4. Negotiation is futile, and you control all the alternatives. _____

C. A Relinquishing style may be effective:

   1. The other person has relevant information which you do not possess. _____

   2. The other person's Child is upset and needs your Nurturing Parent. _____

   3. Development of the other person's autonomy is the most important objective. _____

   4. The other person is autonomous, yet a caring relationship still exists. _____

D. A Defensive style may be effective:

   1. Your Child is confused or frustrated. _____

   2. Participation is against the moral standards of your Parent. _____

   3. Your support is not required. _____

   4. You are aware that games are being played. _____

Fill in the criteria score chart below, Use the criteria score chart to develop a transactional strategy that will effectively attain your Desired Result.

Criteria Score Chart

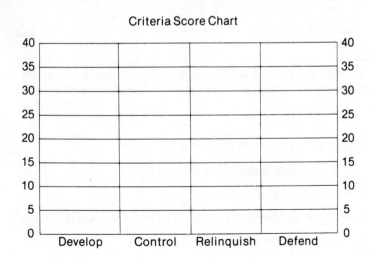

If some other style appears to be close to another one on your chart, you may want to incorporate that in your approach. Both may be appropriate at different times in the dialogue or discussion.

### *Strategy*

1. What style is indicated for your Improved Dialogue?

_____

2. Look over carefully what you have written in Sections I-IX and use it to help yourself decide how to implement that style. Then make some notes on what you will do:

_____

_____

_____

_____

_____

_____

_____

_____

_____

_____

3. When will you do it?  _____

_____

# CHAPTER THREE

# Despite your lousy environment...

**Subject:** Interviewing prospective secretarial employee
**Initiator:** Applicant
**Point of View:** Interviewer
**Desired Result:** a) To obtain sufficient information to make a judgment
        b) To bolster the applicant's desire for the job, if early conversation
            is encouraging as to skill.
**Applicant:** Sarah Gregg      **Interviewer:** Rex Primero

The Bibble Ball Bearing Co. is in the midst of an affirmative action program, having been found to be discriminatory in its personnel practices. Since the salary offered by the Bibble Co. is just about the local average, money isn't a powerful attraction to prospective employees. And Sarah Gregg has one point in her favor to start with. She is black, which in the best of all worlds shouldn't be a factor in considering an employee but in this situation at this time makes her a highly desirable employee for the Bibble Co., especially if her skills are acceptable. She has responded to a newspaper ad and her letter of application was literate and well typed. She walks into the office of Rex Primero with papers in her hand; he rises as she enters, gestures her to a chair in front of the desk, taking the papers from her hand.

**Primero:** Ah, I see you've completed our little typing test, Ms. Gregg.

**Gregg:** Please, it's *Mrs.* Gregg. I haven't accepted that mizz routine. . . I worked hard for my M.R.S. degree!

**Primero:** (*Light laugh*) Of course, of course. . . you have a right to choose the. . . designation that you. . . uh. . . choose. (*Laugh*) Well, now. . . hmmm. . . your typing is apparently somewhat better than average.

**Gregg:** Thank you. I can assure you that I can handle shorthand just as good. . .

**Primero:** Just as *well*, Mrs. Gregg. Oh, sorry—habit. I'm sort of a stickler for grammar.

**Gregg:** In that case, I suppose this job just wouldn't work out for me. . . (*Starts to rise*)

**Primero:** Please, please, stay seated. . . I didn't mean that the way it sounded. I'm perfectly aware that people raised in. . . uh. . . certain. . . uh. . . surroundings. . . sometimes pick up local uh. . . differences in language.

**Gregg:** (*Laughs*) Maybe it ought to be my turn to try to make *you* a bit more comfortable, Mr. Primero. My being black has nothing to do with any grammatical errors I make. My family is strictly middle class, I never lived in the ghetto, and I went to schools that were exactly the same as those everyone who wants to learn secretarial skills goes to. . . you have the record there. . .

**Primero:** Yes, certainly. You do understand that, well, there just aren't enough qualified black people applying for jobs and I wanted to make it clear that. . .

**Gregg:** You have. OK, you know what I can do, do you think I can handle the job?

**Primero:** Quite frankly, yes. How soon can you start, assuming we can iron out the details...

**Gregg:** The details to me are basically money, Mr. Primero. I'm putting my husband through college.

**Primero:** Money is important, I agree. But there's more to it than that. Our fringe benefits include full hospitalization coverage...

**Gregg:** That's nice.

**Primero:** And we will cover one dependent... in this case your husband... uh, that is, unless you have children...

**Gregg:** No. No kids.

**Primero:** Then there's the company cafeteria and free parking...

**Gregg:** Fine, I appreciate all the extras, Mr. Primero... but what does the job pay?

**Primero:** We're right in line here with the prevailing pay scale, Mrs. Gregg. You would start at $600 a month.

**Gregg:** $600. That's about average, all right. What kind of work would I be doing... I mean, who would I be working for?

**Primero:** Our traffic manager, Mr. Buford... he's a fine man to work for, I can assure you... very liberally minded, fair, you know.

**Gregg:** Yeah. I know. Bills of lading, routing sheets, that routine, right?

**Primero:** Yes... it's a great opportunity to learn the field... you know, things like shipping rates, routing, you know...

**Gregg:** Mmm-hmm. And I'm sure there's no barrier around here to advancement for anybody, including minority type folks, right?

**Primero:** Absolutely!

**Gregg:** Mr. Primero, give my regards to the government folks...

**Primero:** What? I mean... What government folks...

**Gregg:** The Fair Employment Practices fuzz... Man, you signal like a traffic light... Tell 'em you really tried but I just didn't appreciate a chance to improve my poor black self. 'Bye.

## ANALYSIS: IGNORING USEFUL INFORMATION
### Interviewing Prospective Secretarial Employee

**Script Theme:** "They're all alike."

**Tapes:** Parent—"Black folks are poor, lazy and shiftless."
        Child —"Bright women are very threatening."

**Key Crossed Transaction:**

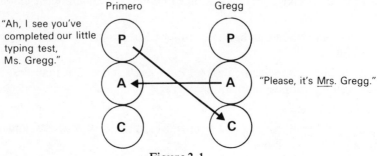

Figure 3.1

*Note*: This is where the dialogue essentially remains throughout, until the end when Sarah finally gives up and responds from her Critical Parent.

**Ulterior Message:** "You don't count and you never will."

**Basic Life Position:** "I'm OK—you're not-OK."

**Game:** *I'm Only Trying to Help You*

**Role:** Rescuer ("Ah, I see you've completed our little typing test, Ms. Gregg.")

Rex Primero is unaware of the influence of his Parent ego state. Evidently it has contaminated his Adult, blocking his ability to perceive or make use of the feedback he gets. Of course, his Parent works just fine if there are other likeminded Parents around. Since they don't have to check any facts they can all heartily agree about things such as women, politics, or employees. Since he leads with his Parent and not his fact-gathering Adult, he is bound to be in trouble with the shrewd, hard-nosed Sarah.

Early in the conversation, he could have easily detected that her Adult was out to protect her interests and her identity. The first sign occurs when she crosses his transaction with her request for being called *Mrs.* Instead of using this as a piece of useful information, however, he tries to gloss it over.

Since he is flying blind as far as the dynamics of the situation are concerned, he immediately falls into the same trap again. Evidently he has already decided that Sarah is not bright and of no consequence. His behavior indicates an attitude of "Let's get this out of the way" or "We're doing this because we have to." His opinions are not based on his own Adult observation in the here and now and his choices are not his own. So, after he corrects her grammar, his attempt to cover up for it only makes matters worse. He has ignored the fact that Sarah is a conservative member of the middle class, which she has already indicated by her statement about being called *Mrs.* What he is "perfectly aware" of in his faltering attempt to cover up his faux pas is merely his script theme, "They're all alike."

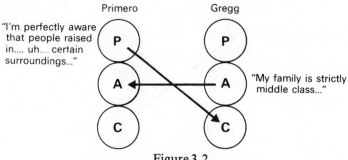

Figure 3.2

He goes on without being sensitive to the fact that Sarah is interested in information about what the job pays, not the fringe benefits. He has completely missed how realistic she is about him and the job. Evidently he thinks of himself as a helpful kind of guy who is giving this poor person who doesn't know any better a break. His Parent tapes, though essentially negative, have some liberal overtones in them about helping poor folks. It doesn't mean granting power to them or anything like that. Their dependent condition gives Rex's Nurturing Parent a sense of being needed, a stroke supply he would be loathe to give up.

Sarah spots his game when she realizes that there would be no future for her in working for the traffic manager. How could she, being a woman, advance in that area? She knows that underneath Mr. Primero's bland assertion that "it's a great opportunity to learn the field" is the secret message that "you don't count." His Nurturing Parent is only a disguise for his Critical Parent—a disguise which does not fool Sarah, who is wise to the ways of Whitey.

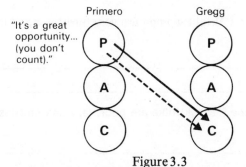

Figure 3.3

She simply does not play the game he invites her to play—which would have ensued had she taken the job. If she had done that, months later she would have realized that he was "only *trying* to help," not *really* helping. She probably then would have become angry and attacked her phoney Rescuer. However, she is too smart for all that. Rather she cuts it short by crossing the transaction from her Critical Parent.

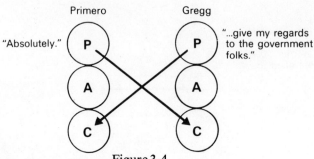

Figure 3.4

She wants a real job, not just a game.

Rex Primero was not aware of what you are aware of now. Be Mr. Primero and rewrite the dialogue, minus the scripting that only blinds his view of reality and reaffirms his Basic Life Position—"I'm OK—you're not-OK." Do one which instead obtains sufficient information to make a judgment, and bolsters the applicant's desire for the job.

## Awareness Format

Revise the script by writing your own version of this dialogue, which has ended so badly. Use the Awareness Format to do it, and then compare your version with ours. A sample for the Awareness Format is provided in the appendix.

### I. Tapes

Change Rex's Child tape ("Bright women are very threatening.") into an Adult statement.

Adult: _____

_____

Change Rex's Parent tape ("Black folks are poor, lazy and shiftless.") into an Adult statement.

Adult: _____

_____

### II. Key Crossed Transaction

Change the crossed transaction (see Fig. 3.1) to make it complementary.

Rex: _____

Sarah: _____

**III. Ulterior Message**
Change Rex's Ulterior Message ("You don't count and you never will.") into an Adult statement.
Adult: _____

_____

**IV. Role**
Change what Rex said in his Rescuer role to an Adult statement.
Rescuer: "Ah, I see you've completed our little typing test, Ms. Gregg."
Adult: _____

_____

**V. Style**
On a scale from 1 to 10 grade the applicability of each criterion from Rex's point of view. (See the introduction to this book for a detailed explanation of the criteria.)

Grade
1 to 10

A. A Developmental style may be effective:

1. The Adult is available in the other person. _____

2. A joint decision is important. _____

3. An impasse has been reached and a new approach is desired. _____

4. There is time for study and discussion. _____

B. A Controlling style may be effective:

1. The chief priority is to get the task done as soon as possible. _____

2. You intend to direct the project in your own way. _____

3. Ready assent is forthcoming from the other person's Child. _____

4. Negotiation is futile, and you control all the alternatives. _____

C. A Relinquishing style may be effective:

1. The other person has relevant information which you do not possess. _____

2. The other person's Child is upset and needs your Nurturing Parent. _____

3. Development of the other person's autonomy is the most important objective. _____

4. The other person is autonomous, yet a caring relationship still exists. _____

D. A Defensive style may be effective:

1. Your Child is confused or frustrated.                          _____

2. Participation is against the moral standards of your Parent.   _____

3. Your support is not required.                                  _____

4. You are aware that games are being played.                     _____

Fill in the criteria score chart below according to the numbers indicated for each style. Use the criteria score chart to select a transactional style which is designed to effectively achieve Rex's Desired Result.

Criteria Score Chart

| 40 | | | | | 40 |
|----|---|---|---|---|----|
| 35 | | | | | 35 |
| 30 | | | | | 30 |
| 25 | | | | | 25 |
| 20 | | | | | 20 |
| 15 | | | | | 15 |
| 10 | | | | | 10 |
| 5 | | | | | 5 |
| 0 | Develop | Control | Relinquish | Defend | 0 |

If another style is graded close to the highest one on your chart, you may want to incorporate that in your approach. Both may be appropriate at different times in the dialogue or discussion.

*Strategy*

1. What style is indicated for the Improved Dialogue? _____

_____

2. Make some notes on how Rex's strategy might be improved, using the style indicated.

_____

_____

_____

_____

———————————————————————

———————————————————————

———————————————————————

Now read the Improved Dialogue and compare it with what you have written in Sections I through V.

## THE IMPROVED DIALOGUE
### Interviewing Applicant for Secretarial Employment

Even after absorbing the TA insights he needs to handle the situation, Rex Primero still is faced with a very difficult task. He needs to be both color-blind and color-conscious at the same time. After getting his Parent tape/stereotype image of blacks subdued, he must bring the fact of the affirmative action program into his Adult consciousness. In essence, on an Adult plane, he needs to make clear to the applicant that with the company's current enlightenment, being black will be an advantage, assuming that skill quotients are equal. Now, we take up the same interview but in this case, Rex Primero has carefully read Sarah Gregg's application, understands her actual environmental background and has, with a very real and conscious effort, convinced his aggressive Parent to stay in the background.

**Primero:** Ah, I see you've completed our little typing test, Ms. Gregg...

**Gregg:** Please, it's *Mrs.* Gregg... I haven't accepted that mizz routine... I worked hard for my M.R.S. degree!

**Primero:** (*Light laugh*) Of course, of course... sometimes we try too hard to keep up with the times, Mrs. Gregg. I'm as guilty as anyone... Mrs. Gregg it is.

**Gregg:** Thank you.

**Primero:** I see from the test that your typing is somewhat better than average...

**Gregg:** Thanks again... and I can assure you that I can handle shorthand just as good...

**Primero:** Just as *well*, Mrs. Gregg... oh, sorry—habit... I'm sort of a stickler for grammer...

**Gregg:** In that case, I suppose this job wouldn't work out for me... (*Starts to rise*)

**Primero:** Please, please stay seated. I didn't mean that the way it sounded. I'm perfectly aware that... (*Laugh*) uh, if I were to use grammar as a criterion, I'd have to fire half my junior executives!

**Gregg:** (*Laugh*) You're also well aware of the fact that I'm black, and I can understand it if you think that my English carries a ghetto influence. It doesn't, and I think it's fair that I assure you of that.

**Primero:** Not necessary. I read your application.

**Gregg:** Fine. Do you think I can handle the job, Mr. Primero?

**Primero:** Yes. What's more, I want you to feel very positive about coming to work with us. I have no doubt we can iron out the details...

**Gregg:** The details are money, basically, Mr. Primero. I'm putting my husband through college.

**Primero:** We're right in line with the prevailing pay scale... You would start at $600 a month.

**Gregg:** That's about average, all right.

**Primero:** I think in fairness to yourself and our company, Mrs. Gregg, you should take into consideration the very liberal fringe benefits including insurance coverage for you and one dependent... in this case your husband... If you have children...

**Gregg:** No, no children.

**Primero:** Then there's the company cafeteria and free parking, all of which has been calculated to add some 12% to the value of your salary... But quite bluntly, in your case there's more to it than all that.

**Gregg:** What do you mean? For example... what kind of work would I do?

**Primero:** The current opening is as secretary to our traffic manager. But this is a large company and your advancement can take place within the department or outside of it. As you pointed out, the fact that you're black could have, in the past, led to stereotyped conclusions about your ability. I'm ashamed to say that it took government action to open this company's eyes, but we are making a real effort to make up for our oversights. That means, in straight-out language, that because you're black and because we're committed to bringing our company's personnel situation up to snuff, your chances for advancement and pay increases are very good indeed.

**Gregg:** You're honest enough, Mr. Primero, and I appreciate that. But since we're speaking so frankly, does that affirmative action plan die as soon as the government stops looking over your shoulder?

**Primero:** No, it does not. For several reasons. First, I hope you will accept my assurances that our actions are based not only on government order but on a plan that we had voluntarily established before the agency got into the act... I guess they felt we weren't moving fast enough and I think they were right. But more than that, people like you will assure our staying on the right track.

**Gregg:** People like me?

**Primero:** Yes. I believe that your performance on the job, assuming it matches your background and obvious ability, will help all of our executives develop a permanent case of color-blindness.

**Gregg:** You can report to those government folks that you're one step forward in the direction they pointed you. When do I start?

## Awareness Format Applied to Your Own Situation

### I. Background
Describe briefly a situation in which you have had a responsible part and are not satisfied with the results:

_____

_____

_____

### II. Desired Result
What was your Desired Result? _____

_____

### III. Key Crossed Transaction
In that situation identify a key crossed transaction in which the response came from the Parent or the Child in the other person.

What you said: _____

_____

The response: _____

_____

Diagram your crossed transaction:

### IV. Tapes
Imagine yourself as you were when you were a very young child and think of an experience which is similar to the one you have just described. Be aware of the people who appear in your mind's eye, what you felt and what you were trying to say to them.

In the recent situation which you have just described, what appears to be the Child tape influencing your behavior from that old scene in your past?

Child tape: _____

_____

Change your Child tape into an Adult statement:

Adult: _____

_____

What appears to be your Parent tape? If you need to, go back to the memory you just retrieved for an awareness of that tape.

Parent tape: _____

_____

Change your Parent tape into an Adult statement:

Adult: _____

_____

## V. Ulterior Message
What Ulterior Message did you send to the other person? You can spot your Ulterior Message by examining your Parent and Child tapes to see how they exerted a negative influence on your transactional style in that situation.

Your Ulterior Message: _____

_____

## VI. Basic Life Position
Check out your feelings in that situation. What Basic Life Position do they seem to indicate?

Check one: ☐ I'm not-OK—you're OK.
           ☐ I'm not-OK—you're not-OK.
           ☐ I'm OK—you're not-OK.
           ☐ I'm OK—you're OK.

What is the feeling? _____

## VII. Game Awareness
Now you can see how the parts of your game fall into place. Write here your Desired Result (see II above).

_____

Write here your Ulterior Message (see V above).

_____

Write here the response you got in the crossed transaction (see III above).

_____

Write here your Basic Life Position in that situation (see VI above) and the feeling that goes with it.

Basic Life Position: _____

Feeling: _____

What game seems to be indicated here?

Name: _____

To get out of that game, change your Ulterior Message in that game into an Adult statement.

Adult: _____

_____

## VIII. Role

What role were you playing in that game? Check one:

☐ Persecutor    ☐ Victim    ☐ Rescuer

Describe what you said or did to play that role.

_____

_____

Change that to an Adult behavior or statement:

Adult: _____

_____

## IX. Style

On a scale from 1 to 10 grade the applicability of each criterion from your point of view. (See the introduction to this book for a detailed explanation of the criteria.)

Grade
1 to 10

A. A Developmental style may be effective:

1. The Adult is available in the other person. _____

2. A joint decision is important. _____

3. An impasse has been reached and a new approach is desired. _____

4. There is time for study and discussion. _____

B. A Controlling style may be effective:

    1. The chief priority is to get the task done as soon as possible.   \_\_\_\_\_

    2. You intend to direct the project in your own way.   \_\_\_\_\_

    3. Ready assent is forthcoming from the other person's Child.   \_\_\_\_\_

    4. Negotiation is futile, and you control all the alternatives.   \_\_\_\_\_

C. A Relinquishing style may be effective:

    1. The other person has relevant information which you do not possess.   \_\_\_\_\_

    2. The other person's Child is upset and needs your Nurturing Parent.   \_\_\_\_\_

    3. Development of the other person's autonomy is the most important objective.   \_\_\_\_\_

    4. The other person is autonomous, yet a caring relationship still exists.   \_\_\_\_\_

D. A Defensive style may be effective:

    1. Your Child is confused or frustrated.   \_\_\_\_\_

    2. Participation is against the moral standards of your Parent.   \_\_\_\_\_

    3. Your support is not required.   \_\_\_\_\_

    4. You are aware that games are being played.   \_\_\_\_\_

Fill in the criteria score chart below, Use the criteria score chart to develop a transactional strategy that will effectively attain your Desired Result.

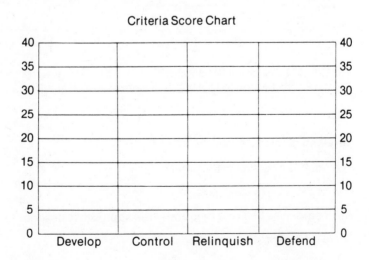

Criteria Score Chart

If some other style appears to be close to another one on your chart, you may want to incorporate that in your approach. Both may be appropriate at different times in the dialogue or discussion.

*Strategy*

1. What style is indicated for your Improved Dialogue?

_____

2. Look over carefully what you have written in Sections I-IX and use it to help yourself decide how to implement that style. Then make some notes on what you will do:

_____

_____

_____

_____

_____

_____

_____

_____

_____

_____

3. When will you do it? _____

_____

# CHAPTER FOUR

# I can play that paper game...

**Subject:** Applying for sales employment
**Initiator:** Applicant
**Point of View:** Applicant
**Desired Result:** a) To get the job
                  b) To get the best commission/salary deal or
                     most lucrative territory
**Applicant:** Clark Burley    **Interviewer:** Lou Watson

Clark Burley has the credentials that identify him as a top notch salesman. By the same token, the Eastwest Manufacturing Company has a reputation for being an ideal employer for salespeople—strong products, enlightened policies, and multiple benefits. This interview takes place in a hotel room in Clark Burley's home town. The Sales Manager, Lou Watson, has come here for the express purpose of interviewing salesmen for this territory. He greets Burley at the door.

**Watson:** Mr. Burley... Come on in, you're right on time.

**Burley:** (*They shake hands*) When a prospect says come on and sell me, I make sure I show up on time! You're Lou Watson, right?

**Watson:** Right. Here, we can sit at this table... (*They sit down facing each other*)

**Burley:** Mr. Watson, I want to say something right up front. You have a great personal reputation in the trade, your company has the same kind of a reputation, and I'm here because I want to work with you. I plan to do a selling job today... and the commodity I have to sell is Clark Burley.

**Watson:** Call me Lou. Listen, let's get some of the nitty-gritty questions out of the way, and then I'll let you tell me why you're the best thing that could happen to Eastwest Manufacturing, OK?

**Burley:** Good enough. Fire away, Lou.

**Watson:** Do you have any problems with being away from home about two weeks out of the month?

**Burley:** No, not as long as I can get home for weekends at least a major part of the time.

**Watson:** Fair enough. Now, as you know, our products are sold for resale...

**Burley:** And the idea is to move them out, not stock them in, right? Listen, I've seen your ads for the Whirlabrush, that revolving broom, and I know that it doesn't do you any good to have them sold into a warehouse somewhere...

**Watson:** Exactly. And that's why our commission setup isn't based on flat volume sales figures...

**Burley:** As long as I can make money by doing a better sales job, it doesn't matter what the bookkeeping system is... (*Laugh*)

**Watson:** Well, it's based on a rolling average per retail outlet... rather a complicated formula, but briefly it's weighted to reflect merchandise moving out of the stores as well as into them.

**Burley:** Fine. Look, I know I can live with the mechanics of the job, so let me get down to the Clark Burley story...

**Watson:** We have a reporting system that requires you to become familiar with several different forms that have to be...

**Burley:** Oh, sure, the old paperwork. (*Laugh*) I'm sure you're much more interested in the bottom line—sales results—than you are in a guy who can make out papers...

**Watson:** Well, we place a good deal of importance on these routine matters...

**Burley:** Sure, Lou, and listen, I can play that paper game... but the important thing is that when I call on an Eastwest customer... or a potential customer, and that's even more important, right?...

**Watson:** Of course, that's important, but corporate routine requires...

**Burley:** Selling isn't routine, Lou, you and I know that! We have to keep the old auditors happy, but sales people march to a different drummer. Now, I can tell you that I was able to increase the volume of...

**Watson:** Hold it. Look, Burley, I appreciate your enthusiasm, but I've got to make sure that I've put the whole job in perspective. Now, let's talk about the reporting system for a few moments.

**Burley:** Oh, yeah, sure... I mean... (*Laugh*) you're looking at an old firehorse answering the bell, Lou.

**Watson:** Certainly. I'll make this shorter than I should... We have a daily and weekly call report, a monthly new placement summary and seven other report forms that you will have to become familiar with if you work with us.

**Burley:** Great, I can handle that as long as the company doesn't judge me on my handwriting instead of my sales! (*Laugh)*

**Watson:** Do you have any questions about the reporting system?

**Burley:** Naw, I can learn the whole thing in a day once I'm in harness. Now, let me tell you about my philosophy of selling... It isn't the run-of-the-mill hard-pitch kind of thing, no sir. What I do when I set up a call...

**Watson:** Do you have any questions about our product line, Burley?

**Burley:** No, sir... I can learn all that on the job... Now here's the Clark Burley story...

**Watson:** OK, you go ahead... I hope you don't mind if I sort of look through these papers while you talk... I'll be listening to you, of course...

## ANALYSIS: THE SECRET SUPERMAN
### Applying for Sales Employment

**Script Theme:** "I can leap tall buildings at a single bound."

**Tapes:** Parent—"Be the best."
       Child —"Just watch me, Dad!"
             "Look, Ma, no hands!"

**Key Crossed Transaction:**

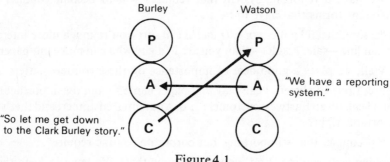

Figure 4.1

**Ulterior Message:** "Winners don't have to bother with minor details (kick me)."

**Basic Life Position:** "I'm OK—you're not-OK," as a cover-up for "I'm not-OK—you're OK."

**Games:** *Mine Is Bigger Than Yours, Kick Me*

**Roles:** Rescuer ("You're looking at an old firehorse answering the bell.")
       Victim ("Salesmen march to a different drummer.")

Clark Burley is out more to save the world than to get the job. His script is based on the story of Superman, who has often tried to do the impossible. As a young child, Clark—or Charlie, as he was called then—found the Superman image useful to identify his parents' expectations. These old tapes still influence his behavior, especially when he is *selling himself.* When a prospect says, "Come on and sell me," Clark Kent (not Clark Burley) responds, and the "me" that is sold is not the client but Superman. To a little boy's world it made sense; to grownups it is simply unrealistic and inappropriate. In some ways this game is useful in dealing with Clark's fears that he may not be all that he's cracked up to be, because his game pretends that he is bigger and better than anyone else; but it does not solve his real problem. It simply covers it up. Those not-OK feelings of inferiority are still there. Unfortunately, when he was little, his Adult did not have enough proficiency to check out just how realistic those expectations of his parents were. If his Adult were to do that now, it would be most useful to Clark Burley and probably the end of the Clark Kent image inside him. His enthusiasm could then be realistic (Adult) as well as turned on (Child).

Lou Watson responds with his realistic, fact-gathering Adult early in the conversation, but Clark's psychic energy is all in his Child. (Clark's enthusiasm probably *does* help a lot of times when it comes to promoting sales, but clearly it is not useful in organizing details.)

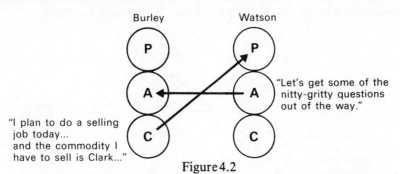

Figure 4.2

Lou Watson knows that he must give direct, clear, specific information to Clark about the expectations of the job, yet he does not once hook Clark's Adult.

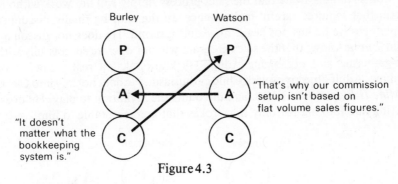

Figure 4.3

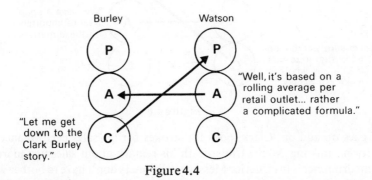

Figure 4.4

Here is the climax of the scene. The communications have broken down because they are talking past each other.

Clark is discounting Lou's Adult. A discount leaves the other person feeling rejected, unwanted, and unstroked. That is the last thing Clark really wants. After all, his desired objective is to get the job and the best deal. But what he doesn't stroke he doesn't get. If his Adult were activated he would be aware of what Lou's Adult is asking for. Instead he vainly tries to hook Lou's Parent with his Child.

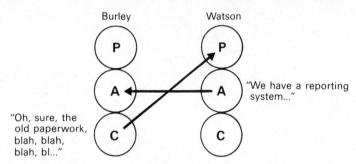

Figure 4.5

Lou's Adult is aware that the sales process simply will not work without a good system that requires careful maintenance. In the end, he finally discounts Clark, simply because he has not heard his Adult respond. He does not discount Clark's Child, but he knows that the sales program will not operate successfully without the fact-gathering and organizing Adult. He knows that a real winner is one who combines Adult objectivity with Child enthusiasm. He does not buy into Clark's game of *Mine Is Bigger than Yours*, and discounts the invitation to play. He does this by offering and looking for only the strokes that are acceptable to him.

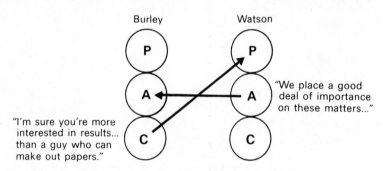

Figure 4.6

It goes on and on. Clark looks for strokes for his sales performance and Lou looks for his missing Adult. Underneath his remark about salesmen marching to a different drummer is his Ulterior Message, "Winners don't have to bother with minor details." Lou is aware of that message and in the end responds to it by rejecting Clark. This amounts to a game of *Kick Me* in which the final rejection is the kick. At that point Clark changes from the role of Rescuer to Victim.

Clark's script of leaping tall buildings is really a loser's script, not a winner's. The leap he makes is not over them but down them, from the false heights of his ego. Without paying attention to the objective facts of the sales reporting system and the product line, he would simply be doing the same old thing on the job that he'd always done. He'd be saying "Gee, aren't I wonderful?" and the important information about the product line and how the sales campaign developed would be lost.

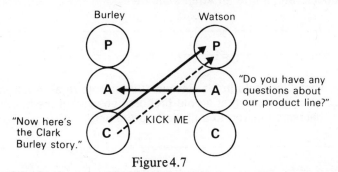

Figure 4.7

The kick, addressed to the Ulterior Message, is: "...I hope you don't mind if I sort of look through these papers while we talk."

Clark's game of *Kick Me,* which is the one that ties in with his script, would create losses not only for himself, but for the Eastwest Manufacturing Company as well. The "sound of a different drummer" would lead, not to a glamorous end, but rather to professional suicide.

If you were Clark, knowing what you do now, how would you rewrite his encounter with Lou Watson?

## Awareness Format

Revise the script by writing your own version of this dialogue, which has ended so badly. Use the Awareness Format to do it, and then compare your version with ours. A sample for the Awareness Format is provided in the appendix.

### I. Tapes
Change Clark's Child tape ("Just watch me, Dad!" "Look, Ma, no hands!") into an Adult statement.

Adult: _____

_____

### II. Key Crossed Transaction
Change the crossed transaction (see Fig. 4.1) to make it complementary.

Clark: _____

_____

Lou: _____

_____

## III. Ulterior Message

Change Clark's Ulterior Message ("Winners don't have to bother with minor details (kick me).") into an Adult statement.

Adult: _____

_____

## IV. Role

Change what Clark said in his Rescuer/Victim role to an Adult statement.
Rescuer: "You're looking at an old firehorse answering the bell."
Victim: "Salesmen march to a different drummer."

Adult: _____

_____

## V. Style

On a scale from 1 to 10 grade the applicability of each criterion from Clark's point of view. (See the introduction to this book for a detailed explanation of the criteria.)

Grade
1 to 10

A. A Developmental style may be effective:

1. The Adult is available in the other person. _____

2. A joint decision is important. _____

3. An impasse has been reached and a new approach is desired. _____

4. There is time for study and discussion. _____

B. A Controlling style may be effective:

1. The chief priority is to get the task done as soon as possible. _____

2. You intend to direct the project in your own way. _____

3. Ready assent is forthcoming from the other person's Child. _____

4. Negotiation is futile, and you control all the alternatives. _____

C. A Relinquishing style may be effective:

1. The other person has relevant information which you do not possess. _____

2. The other person's Child is upset and needs your Nurturing Parent. _____

3. Development of the other person's autonomy is the most important objective. _____

4. The other person is autonomous, yet a caring relationship still exists.    _____

D. A Defensive style may be effective:

1. Your Child is confused or frustrated.    _____

2. Participation is against the moral standards of your Parent.    _____

3. Your support is not required.    _____

4. You are aware that games are being played.    _____

Fill in the criteria score chart below according to the numbers indicated for each style. Use the criteria score chart to select a transactional style which is designed to effectively achieve Clark's Desired Result.

Criteria Score Chart

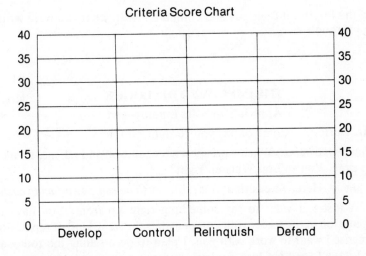

If another style is graded close to the highest one on your chart, you may want to incorporate that in your approach. Both may be appropriate at different times in the dialogue or discussion.

*Strategy*

1. What style is indicated for the Improved Dialogue?    _____

_____

2. Make some notes on how Clark's strategy might be improved, using the same style indicated.

_____

_____

_____

Now read the Improved Dialogue and compare it with what you have written in Sections I through V.

## THE IMPROVED DIALOGUE
### Applying for Sales Employment

**Watson:** Mr. Burley... Come on in, you're right on time.

**Burley:** (*They shake hands*) When a prospect says come on and sell me, I make sure I show up on time. You're Lou Watson, right?

**Watson:** Right... Here, we can sit at this table... (*They sit down facing each other*)

**Burley:** Mr. Watson, I want to say something right up front. You have a great personal reputation in the trade, your company has the same kind of reputation, and I'm here because I want to work with you. I plan to do a selling job today and the commodity I have to sell is Clark Burley.

**Watson:** Call me Lou. Listen. Let's get some of the nitty-gritty things out of the way and then I'll let you tell me why you're the best thing that could happen to Eastwest Manufacturing, OK?

**Burley:** Good enough. Fire away, Lou.

**Watson:** Do you have any problems with being away from home two weeks out of the month?

**Burley:** No, not as long as I can get home for weekends a major part of the time.

**Watson:** Fair enough, now as you know our products are sold for resale.

**Burley:** Yes.

**Watson:** And, since the idea is to move them *through* and not merely *to* retailers, our commission setup isn't based on flat volume sales figures.

**Burley:** Sort of in general terms, what is the setup? I'm interested in a deal that will reflect the results of my ability and efforts...

**Watson:** It's based on a rolling average per outlet and is weighted to reflect merchandise moving out of the stores as well as into them.

**Burley:** I can understand that. You're not looking for a stuffed pipeline that can't digest any more merchandise... If you'll check my resume you'll see that I've got a good track record in merchandising as well as sales... I can do very well under a commission setup like that.

**Watson:** OK. We have a reporting system that requires you to become familiar with several different forms that have to be...

**Burley:** Oh, sure, the old paperwork... excuse me for interrupting... but like any salesman, I have that gut feeling that the bottom line is the most important thing. That doesn't mean I ignore or treat routine reporting lightly...

**Watson:** Fine. We have a weekly call report, a monthly new placement summary and seven other report forms that you will have to become familiar with if you work with us.

**Burley:** Reports are a traditional hangup with sales types, Lou, and I admit it. But I've worked with reporting systems in the past and a good one means my calls are better organized and there's more money in my pocket, so I'm all for 'em. If you decide that you want me to come aboard, I hope you'll spend the time we need for me to get straight on all of them.

**Watson:** That's an honest approach... One more thing, do you have any questions about our product line?

**Burley:** Probably hundreds, Lou! Fact is, I studied some of your literature before I came up here and I'm particularly impressed with the Whirlabrush. But I hope a tour of the plant and an education in the line is part of the indoctrination setup! I'm aware that basically we deal with a housewares specialty line sold through traditional outlets with a heavy push into food stores... but I need to know more.

**Watson:** A complete product line education is part of the first week's training we give to all new men. Of course, I don't think you'll need basic selling technique instruction, but we will... that is, we would... run you through our full two-week course at full draw just for the sake of familiarity with our methods.

**Burley:** OK... Now... I want you to know that my selling philosophy is a lot like the way this interview has been going, Lou. I listen to what the customer's needs and interests are and I try to answer them... and then I close. You read my track record... Am I the man that can fill the bill for you?

**Watson:** If we can get together on money basics, I think it's pretty likely!

**Burley:** Fine. Now, let me start by listening again... What does that rolling average commission translate to in money?

## Awareness Format Applied to Your Own Situation

### I. Background
Describe briefly a situation in which you have had a responsible part and are not satisfied with the results:

_____

_____

_____

### II. Desired Result
What was your Desired Result? _____

_____

### III. Key Crossed Transaction
In that situation identify a key crossed transaction in which the response came from the Parent or the Child in the other person.

What you said: _____

_____

The response: _____

_____

Diagram your crossed transaction:

### IV. Tapes
Imagine yourself as you were when you were a very young child and think of an experience which is similar to the one you have just described. Be aware of the people who appear in your mind's eye, what you felt and what you were trying to say to them.

In the recent situation which you have just described, what appears to be the Child tape influencing your behavior from that old scene in your past?

Child tape: _____

_____

Change your Child tape into an Adult statement:

Adult: _____

_____

What appears to be your Parent tape? If you need to, go back to the memory you just retrieved for an awareness of that tape.

Parent tape: _____

_____

Change your Parent tape into an Adult statement:

Adult: _____

_____

## V. Ulterior Message

What Ulterior Message did you send to the other person? You can spot your Ulterior Message by examining your Parent and Child tapes to see how they exerted a negative influence on your transactional style in that situation.

Your Ulterior Message: _____

_____

## VI. Basic Life Position

Check out your feelings in that situation. What Basic Life Position do they seem to indicate?

Check one: ☐ I'm not-OK—you're OK.
           ☐ I'm not-OK—you're not-OK.
           ☐ I'm OK—you're not-OK.
           ☐ I'm OK—you're OK.

What is the feeling? _____

## VII. Game Awareness

Now you can see how the parts of your game fall into place. Write here your Desired Result (see II above).

_____

Write here your Ulterior Message (see V above).

_____

Write here the response you got in the crossed transaction (see III above).

_____

Write here your Basic Life Position in that situation (see VI above) and the feeling that goes with it.

Basic Life Position:_____

Feeling:  _____

What game seems to be indicated here?

Name:  _____

To get out of that game, change your Ulterior Message in that game into an Adult statement.

Adult:  _____

_____

VIII. **Role**

What role were you playing in that game? Check one:

☐ Persecutor    ☐ Victim    ☐ Rescuer

Describe what you said or did to play that role.

_____

_____

Change that to an Adult behavior or statement:

Adult:  _____

_____

IX. **Style**

On a scale from 1 to 10 grade the applicability of each criterion from your point of view. (See the introduction to this book for a detailed explanation of the criteria.)

Grade
1 to 10

A. A Developmental style may be effective:

1. The Adult is available in the other person.    _____

2. A joint decision is important.    _____

3. An impasse has been reached and a new approach is desired.    _____

4. There is time for study and discussion.    _____

B. A Controlling style may be effective:

  1. The chief priority is to get the task done as soon as possible. _____

  2. You intend to direct the project in your own way. _____

  3. Ready assent is forthcoming from the other person's Child. _____

  4. Negotiation is futile, and you control all the alternatives. _____

C. A Relinquishing style may be effective:

  1. The other person has relevant information which you do not possess. _____

  2. The other person's Child is upset and needs your Nurturing Parent. _____

  3. Development of the other person's autonomy is the most important objective. _____

  4. The other person is autonomous, yet a caring relationship still exists. _____

D. A Defensive style may be effective:

  1. Your Child is confused or frustrated. _____

  2. Participation is against the moral standards of your Parent. _____

  3. Your support is not required. _____

  4. You are aware that games are being played. _____

Fill in the criteria score chart below, Use the criteria score chart to develop a transactional strategy that will effectively attain your Desired Result.

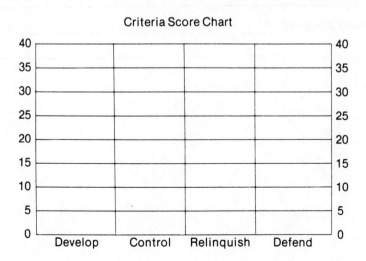

Criteria Score Chart

If some other style appears to be close to another one on your chart, you may want to incorporate that in your approach. Both may be appropriate at different times in the dialogue or discussion.

*Strategy*

1. What style is indicated for your Improved Dialogue?

_____

2. Look over carefully what you have written in Sections I-IX and use it to help yourself decide how to implement that style. Then make some notes on what you will do:

_____

_____

_____

_____

_____

_____

_____

_____

_____

3. When will you do it?  _____

_____

# CHAPTER FIVE

# It was a real hard-sell business . . .

**Subject:** Interviewing prospective sales employee
**Initiator:** Interviewer
**Point of View:** Interviewer
**Desired Result:** a) To get enough information to make a logical judgment
　　　　　　　　b) To bolster the applicant's enthusiasm for the job
**Applicant:** Amanda Paragon　　**Interviewer:** Carlton Lumpert

Carlton Lumpert, of Creative Bank Promotions, Inc., has culled through some thirty applications for the sales position his company advertised. He has selected only a few who appear to be best suited for the job. Amanda Paragon is one of those few, and Lumpert has called her and asked her to show up for an interview. Her written resume was well prepared and thorough, so Lumpert has substantial information about her business background. They are seated opposite each other in Lumpert's office.

**Paragon:** I appreciate your arranging this interview for a Saturday morning, Mr. Lumpert. While I'm looking for a chance to do a bit better, I feel that I owe my full working time to the job I currently hold.

**Lumpert:** I wish more people had that attitude, Ms. Paragon. Now, your resume is pretty complete, so I won't waste our time by asking you questions about your past employment. I would say we can stipulate that it's impressive and that, in general terms, it fits into our needs.

**Paragon:** Thank you.

**Lumpert:** You're currently selling premiums, I see. Can you tell me why you are interested in a change?

**Paragon:** For one thing, the obvious... Your job has more money potential.

**Lumpert:** I think you ought to be aware that the word potential has to be emphasized. I note that your current salary is just about what our salary offer for this job is...

**Paragon:** That's true, but the commission is at a higher percentage. There's more to it than that, though. You see, while I now sell ideas in the form of gifts, merchandise and the like, with your setup I'd be getting involved in the creative end of the business. You offer banks complete packages including printed material, point-of-purchase displays and creative services. I find that challenging and exciting.

**Lumpert:** I'm delighted to see that you show a good understanding of our business, Ms. Paragon. You know, I started in the premium end of the business. Some ten years ago.

**Paragon:** Then you can see the logical step involved for me...

**Lumpert:** Oh, sure thing. Listen, do you remember the old Superpush Premium Company? I was with them when Harry Super himself was still running the show.

**Paragon:** I've heard of them...

**Lumpert:** Let me tell you, it was a real hard-sell business then! Old Harry used to say to me, Carl, oh, listen call me Carl, can I call you Amanda?

**Paragon:** Certainly. I have a couple of questions about the use of the company car and the accounts I'd be assigned...

**Lumpert:** Of course, of course. I'll answer all of your questions. Well, at old Superpush the name of the game was volume... and I can remember one time when I called on this hardnut guy... I think his name was Beatty or Bailey or something like that...

**Paragon:** From what I can see, I have no doubt if anyone could make the sale, you could, Carl. Listen, about the company car...

**Lumpert:** We have a really liberal policy on cars, Amanda. Just turn in your gas receipts, they get paid. No limit on where or how you drive... You settle the personal driving thing with Uncle Sam yourself... We consider it a sort of fringe benefit. How's that?

**Paragon:** Sounds fine. About accounts...

**Lumpert:** Oh, you'll have all you can handle...

**Paragon:** Would I have exclusivity in my territory?

**Lumpert:** Amanda, if you can sell the accounts we give you, you'll do all right, I can tell you. Say, does the Biggapak Company still push those paper bag premiums they used to have? I'll bet they do. Ha... Listen, let me tell you about the time I sold a giant yoyo as a premium to this investment house....

**Paragon:** Then I wouldn't have exclusivity, would I?

**Lumpert:** Well, yes and no. I mean, we'd work that out... There are some house accounts that we've been selling for a long time...

**Paragon:** I see. Can we take a look at the account list and see which accounts are house?

**Lumpert:** Oh, I assure you that won't affect your income. Have I told you that we prepare full presentations for your potential customers?... You know, complete color roughs and copy on a spec basis...

**Paragon:** That's good. Who handles the house accounts?

**Lumpert:** I do that personally. Now then, when would you be available if we decided that...

**Paragon:** I'd have to give a month's notice... But before we take that step, I have several other interviews that I should go to before I make a decision. I'll call you.

## ANALYSIS: A SUSPICIOUS AND TYRANNICAL PARENT
### Interviewing Prospective Sales Employee

**Script Theme:** "Those were the days."

**Tapes:** Parent—"Don't tell outsiders anything about the family."

Child —"Some day I'll be big enough to make lots of friends."

**Key Crossed Transaction:**

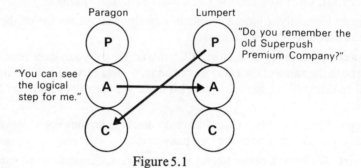

Figure 5.1

**Ulterior Message:** "The important options are in my control."

**Basic Life Position:** "I'm OK—you're not-OK"

**Game:** *I'm Only Trying to Help You*

**Role:** Rescuer ("Well, yes and no, I mean we'd work that out...")

Like the wolf in the Little Red Riding Hood story, old Carlton Lumpert appears to be a folksy friend. He's happy to get friendly with nice girls who bring him goodies but, like the story, it is all a ruse. Beneath that charming appearance there is an avaricious, tyrannical Parent who preys on innocent victims. Amanda doesn't fall for any of it and his Adult is too unaware to see even that. His Parent runs the show for him and his Adult is left out in the cold. His Child goes along with the Parent.

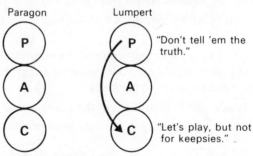

Figure 5.2

What he does in the end is to get rid of Amanda and so fail to obtain his Desired Result. Evidently, Carlton grew up in a very tight-lipped environment. The family didn't have much luck with other folks. They were suspicious and did not want to invest themselves socially or in business for fear of getting ripped off. They were OK, but nobody else was. Carlton learned early in life to cover up these family traits with a mask of cordiality. That way he satisfied his Parent, and his Child could pick up some crumbs. The mask got him some friendly strokes and yet, in back of it, he was not giving anything away. If people saw what he really was, he wouldn't get any strokes at all. He would be just pushing papers, which is the only area in which his Adult is allowed to function because it means no contact with anyone else. Only then does the Parent give permission because there is nothing to lose. He can read Amanda's resume, but not what she's communicating to him through the dialogue.

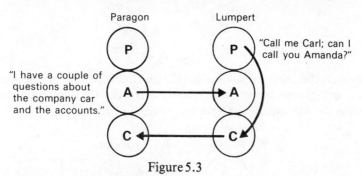

Figure 5.3

Carlton is coming from a tightly controlling Parent but it appears that he is coming from his Child.

The reality of the situation would indicate a diagram like this:

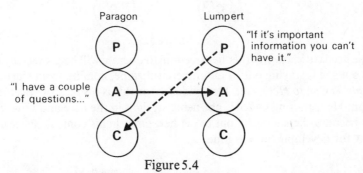

Figure 5.4

He does indeed come out from in back of his smoke screen to tell Amanda about the liberal policy on the use of company cars. Here he can afford to be generous, because it is not an important issue. She registers the information, but goes after the crucial matter of how the accounts are to be handled. The situation is at a point where she can explore what will happen. The options are still hers and she has some choice in the matter. The decision she makes will lead her into either a relationship which allows her to develop and have a high level of commitment or one which forces her to comply and adapt to someone else, who has the advantage. Fortunately for her, she has her Adult up front checking things out. Old Carlton is not operating the same way at all. Coming from his Parent, he generalizes, tells war stories, avoids specifics.

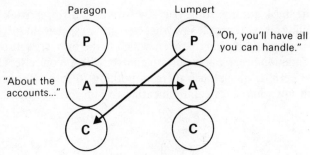

Figure 5.5

If she buys that, she will have to go into her Child ego state and accommodate to the kind of ungenerous power Carlton has to offer. But she is too smart for that. She drives home for the specific information, staying in her Adult.

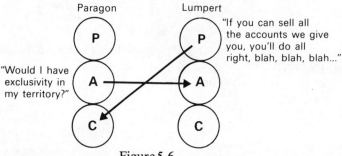

Figure 5.6

She needs to know whether her freedom to operate will be protected. By checking things out she is staying out of an unmerciful game, coming from Carlton, which is *I'm Only Trying to Help You*. Her evidence for this is his lack of specific agreement early on. He is putting her off, not being straight in the here and now. Secretly this folksy friend of hers is really out to get her. Once in his control, she senses that her options for development are gone.

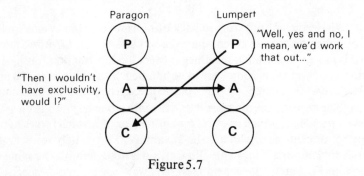

Figure 5.7

Carlton's Rescuing game is not fooling her at all. She knows that a Rescuer needs a Victim and she's not interested in being put in that position. She uses her Adult to protect her Child and is aware that she will not get any protection from him. The same Adult that caused her to look for a better position is now operating to make certain whether it really is better or not. But the information she needs is not forthcoming and she takes note of that.

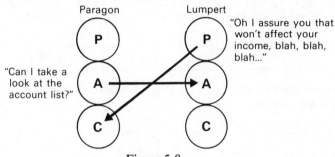

Figure 5.8

The crossed transaction indicates to her that they are really out of communication entirely. But she persists and finally gets the answer.

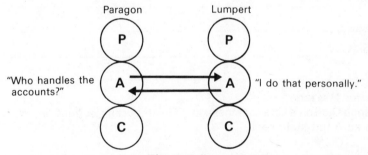

Figure 5.9

This is a complementary transaction and on it the action pivots, bringing about her decision. At last she has gotten a fact out of Carlton. She also knows by this time that in back of that fact there are a host of others about his controlling Parent and his deceitful Child. She senses, too, that once in his control she would be powerless to defend herself against a hefty game on his part of *Now I've Got You, You Little Bitch*. The job does not offer her autonomy or potency, only helpless dependency and a false kind of intimacy. To take it she'd have to be desperate for security. But there is nothing in her makeup that fits into Carlton's script. His dilemma is that he wants a bright employee, but anyone who is that bright is bound to see through him.

Knowing these things, how would you revise the dialogue to get enough information to make a logical judgment and to bolster the enthusiasm of an applicant of the kind you want?

## Awareness Format

Revise the script by writing your own version of this dialogue, which has ended so badly. Use the Awareness Format to do it, and then compare your version with ours. A sample for the Awareness Format is provided in the appendix.

### I. Tapes
Change Carlton's Child tape ("Some day I'll be big enough to make lots of friends.") into an Adult statement.

Adult: _____

_____

Change Carlton's Parent tape ("Don't tell outsiders anything about the family.") into an Adult statement.

Adult: _____

_____

### II. Key Crossed Transaction
Change the crossed transaction (see Fig. 5.1) to make it complementary.

Carlton: _____

_____

Amanda: _____

_____

### III. Ulterior Message
Change Carlton's Ulterior Message ("The important options are in my control.") into an Adult statement.

Adult: _____

_____

### IV. Role
Change what Carlton said in his Rescuer role to an Adult statement.
Rescuer: "Well, yes and no, I mean we'd work that out..."

Adult: _____

_____

_____

## V. Style

On a scale from 1 to 10 grade the applicability of each criterion from Carlton's point of view. (See the introduction to this book for a detailed explanation of the criteria.)

Grade
1 to 10

A. A Developmental style may be effective:

1. The Adult is available in the other person.  _____

2. A joint decision is important.  _____

3. An impasse has been reached and a new approach is desired.  _____

4. There is time for study and discussion.  _____

B. A Controlling style may be effective:

1. The chief priority is to get the task done as soon as possible.  _____

2. You intend to direct the project in your own way.  _____

3. Ready assent is forthcoming from the other person's Child.  _____

4. Negotiation is futile, and you control all the alternatives.  _____

C. A Relinquishing style may be effective:

1. The other person has relevant information which you do not possess.  _____

2. The other person's Child is upset and needs your Nurturing Parent.  _____

3. Development of the other person's autonomy is the most important objective.  _____

4. The other person is autonomous, yet a caring relationship still exists.  _____

D. A Defense style may be effective:

1. Your Child is confused or frustrated.  _____

2. Participation is against the moral standards of your Parent.  _____

3. Your support is not required.  _____

4. You are aware that games are being played.  _____

Fill in the criteria score chart below according to the numbers indicated for each style. Use the criteria score chart to select a transactional style which is designed to effectively achieve Carlton's Desired Result.

Criteria Score Chart

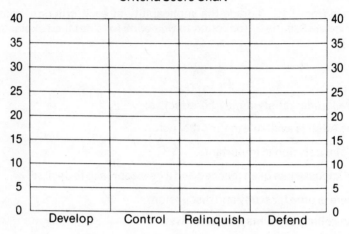

If another style is graded close to the highest one on your chart, you may want to incorporate that in your approach. Both may be appropriate at different times in the dialogue or discussion.

*Strategy*

1. What style is indicated for the Improved Dialogue? _____

_____

2. Make some notes on how Carlton's strategy might be improved, using the style indicated.

_____

_____

_____

_____

_____

_____

_____

_____

_____

Now read the Improved Dialogue and compare it with what you have written in Sections I through V.

### THE IMPROVED DIALOGUE
#### Interviewing Prospective Sales Employee

The smokescreen that Carlton generates as he avoids direct answers is so important to his self-esteem that its content cannot be killed even after he becomes aware of the TA ramifications of the transaction. It is fairly self-evident that with her complete resume and her answers to the first couple of questions, Carlton has gotten quite enough information to make a logical judgment—that she is eminently suited to the job. His struggle is with part (b) of the Desired Result—to bolster the applicant's enthusiasm—and this is where, were his Adult in control, he could throw out his little personal stroke-magnets and still keep on a reasonably complementary transaction level... like this:

**Paragon:** I appreciate your arranging this interview for a Saturday morning, Mr. Lumpert. While I'm looking for a chance to do a bit better, I feel that I owe my full working time to the job that I currently hold.

**Lumpert:** I wish more people had that attitude, Ms. Paragon. Now, your resume is pretty complete so I won't waste your time by asking you questions about your past employment. I would say that we can stipulate that it's impressive and that, in general terms, it fits into our needs.

**Paragon:** Thank you.

**Lumpert:** You're currently selling premiums, I see. Can you tell me why you're interested in a change?

**Paragon:** For one thing, the obvious. Your job has more money potential.

**Lumpert:** I think you ought to be aware that the word potential has to be emphasized. I note that your current salary is just about what our salary offer for this job is...

**Paragon:** That's true, but the commission is at a higher percentage. There's more to it than that, though. You see, while I now sell ideas in the form of gifts, merchandise and the like, with your setup I'd be getting involved in the creative end of the business. You offer banks complete packages including printed material, point-of-purchase displays and creative services. I find that challenging and exciting.

**Lumpert:** I'm delighted to see that you show a good understanding of our business, Ms. Paragon. You know, I started in the premium end of the business some ten years ago...

**Paragon:** Then you can see the logical step involved for me...

**Lumpert:** Oh, sure thing. Listen, do you remember the old Superpush Premium Company? I was with them when Harry Super was still running the show...

**Paragon:** I've heard of them.

**Lumpert:** Let me tell you—well, just to underscore that I understand how the premium end of the business is, you know—I can remember it was hard sell in those days! Some day I hope I get the chance to tell you about some of the hard nuts he had me calling on!

**Paragon:** Premiums are a bit harder sell than a full creative service, I'll agree. I have a couple of questions about the use of the company car and the accounts I'd be assigned...

**Lumpert:** Of course... Shall I start with the car?

**Paragon:** Fine.

**Lumpert:** We have a really liberal policy there. Just turn in your gas receipts and they get paid. No limit on where or how you drive... You settle the personal driving thing with Uncle Sam yourself... We consider it a sort of fringe benefit... How's that?

**Paragon:** Sounds fine. About accounts...

**Lumpert:** Oh, you'll have all you can handle.

**Paragon:** Will I have exclusivity in my territory?

**Lumpert:** Yes, you will, except for eight accounts that I handle personally and have handled for about eight years. I'm sure you understand... One of those accounts, an investment house, is a place where the first thing I sold them was, would you believe, a giant yoyo...

**Paragon:** In other words, you will list eight specific accounts that are house and all the rest in the territory are exclusively mine?

**Lumpert:** Every one. You get paid the commission no matter how the orders come in.

**Paragon:** I can live with that... as long as the accounts on your list aren't the only good accounts in the territory.

**Lumpert:** Here it is. (*Laughs*) That investment house is really the only big one... (*He hands her a list*) and maybe it's ego but these people are old timers who I really believe prefer to do business with me on an old-buddy basis, you know. Remember, we prepare full presentations on spec for your own prospects... besides the accounts we turn over. And if there's an account or two outside your territory that you've established a good relationship with, we can work them into your list too.

**Paragon:** Sounds fair. I'd need two weeks to give my current employer notice... that is, if you feel that...

**Lumpert:** Come on aboard, Ms. Paragon! Say, can I call you Amanda?

## Awareness Format Applied to Your Own Situation

### I. Background
Describe briefly a situation in which you have had a responsible part and are not satisfied with the results:

_____

_____

_____

### II. Desired Result
What was your Desired Result? _____

_____

### III. Key Crossed Transaction
In that situation identify a key crossed transaction in which the response came from the Parent or the Child in the other person.

What you said: _____

_____

The response: _____

_____

Diagram your crossed transaction:

### IV. Tapes
Imagine yourself as you were when you were a very young child and think of an experience which is similar to the one you have just described. Be aware of the people who appear in your mind's eye, what you felt and what you were trying to say to them.

In the recent situation which you have just described, what appears to be the Child tape influencing your behavior from that old scene in your past?

Child tape: _____

_____

Change your Child tape into an Adult statement:

Adult: _____

_____

What appears to be your Parent tape? If you need to, go back to the memory you just retrieved for an awareness of that tape.

Parent tape: _____

_____

Change your Parent tape into an Adult statement:

Adult: _____

_____

## V.  Ulterior Message
What Ulterior Message did you send to the other person? You can spot your Ulterior Message by examining your Parent and Child tapes to see how they exerted a negative influence on your transactional style in that situation.

Your Ulterior Message: _____

_____

## VI.  Basic Life Position
Check out your feelings in that situation. What Basic Life Position do they seem to indicate?

Check one:  ☐ I'm not-OK—you're OK.
☐ I'm not-OK—you're not-OK.
☐ I'm OK—you're not-OK.
☐ I'm OK—you're OK.

What is the feeling? _____

## VII.  Game Awareness
Now you can see how the parts of your game fall into place. Write here your Desired Result (see II above).

_____

Write here your Ulterior Message (see V above).

_____

Write here the response you got in the crossed transaction (see III above).

_____

Write here your Basic Life Position in that situation (see VI above) and the feeling that goes with it.

Basic Life Position:_____

Feeling:    _____

What game seems to be indicated here?

Name:    _____

To get out of that game, change your Ulterior Message in that game into an Adult statement.

Adult:    _____

_____

## VIII. Role

What role were you playing in that game? Check one:

☐ Persecutor    ☐ Victim    ☐ Rescuer

Describe what you said or did to play that role.

_____

_____

Change that to an Adult behavior or statement:

Adult:    _____

_____

## IX. Style

On a scale from 1 to 10 grade the applicability of each criterion from your point of view. (See the introduction to this book for a detailed explanation of the criteria.)

Grade
1 to 10

A. A Developmental style may be effective:

1. The Adult is available in the other person.    _____

2. A joint decision is important.    _____

3. An impasse has been reached and a new approach is desired.    _____

4. There is time for study and discussion.    _____

B. A Controlling style may be effective:

   1. The chief priority is to get the task done as soon as possible.   _____

   2. You intend to direct the project in your own way.   _____

   3. Ready assent is forthcoming from the other person's Child.   _____

   4. Negotiation is futile, and you control all the alternatives.   _____

C. A Relinquishing style may be effective:

   1. The other person has relevant information which you do not possess.   _____

   2. The other person's Child is upset and needs your Nurturing Parent.   _____

   3. Development of the other person's autonomy is the most important objective.   _____

   4. The other person is autonomous, yet a caring relationship still exists.   _____

D. A Defensive style may be effective:

   1. Your Child is confused or frustrated.   _____

   2. Participation is against the moral standards of your Parent.   _____

   3. Your support is not required.   _____

   4. You are aware that games are being played.   _____

Fill in the criteria score chart below, Use the criteria score chart to develop a transactional strategy that will effectively attain your Desired Result.

Criteria Score Chart

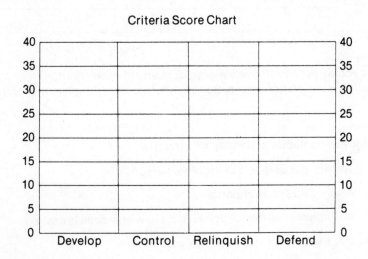

If some other style appears to be close to another one on your chart, you may want to incorporate that in your approach. Both may be appropriate at different times in the dialogue or discussion.

*Strategy*

1. What style is indicated for your Improved Dialogue?

_____

2. Look over carefully what you have written in Sections I-IX and use it to help yourself decide how to implement that style. Then make some notes on what you will do:

_____
_____
_____
_____
_____
_____
_____
_____
_____
_____

3. When will you do it? _____

_____

# SECTION TWO

# Change in employment status

# CHAPTER SIX

# It's because of the Plastergild account...

**Subject:** Seeking a pay raise
**Initiator:** Employee
**Point of View:** Employee
**Desired Result:** Higher salary without ill-feeling
**Employee:** Emanuel Worthy    **Employer (immediate superior):** Frank Harlow

Greenspan, Garfinkle, Abernathy, Biddle and Veurst Advertising (known as "Two Gees and a Beevee" or "Two Gees") is a large agency. Frank Harlow is Vice President, Creative Services and Emanuel Worthy is Creative Director. Worthy is at the open door of Harlow's office.

**Worthy:** Say, Frank, can I talk to you for a couple of minutes?

**Harlow:** Sure. Come on in... I've got about twenty minutes before a policy meeting upstairs.

**Worthy:** Swell. (*Goes into the office*) Mind if I close the door? This is personal...

**Harlow:** Go ahead. Sit down and tell me what's on your mind.

**Worthy:** Thanks. It's money, Frank.

**Harlow:** (*Laugh*) That's pretty much on everyone's mind nowadays, isn't it?

**Worthy:** Listen, it's no laughing matter, Frank. I'm pretty serious about this.

**Harlow:** OK, OK, Manny, I didn't mean for it to sound that way.

**Worthy:** Look, I do a pretty good job around here, right?

**Harlow:** I have no major complaints.

**Worthy:** Well, I haven't had a raise in a year. I think I'm about due, it's just as simple as that, Frank.

**Harlow:** Put on that basis, Manny, let me be straight with you... There haven't been many raises in this shop for the past 12-14 months. You know what business has been like.

**Worthy:** Say, does that mean you're giving me a flat no before we even talk about it, Frank?

**Harlow:** That isn't what I said, Manny. I was explaining the situation.

**Worthy:** I guess it's because of the Plastergild account, isn't it?

**Harlow:** I don't understand.

**Worthy:** I think you do. Come on, Frank, we can talk frankly, can't we? I mean, I know we had a conflict on the Plastergild presentation...

**Harlow:** Yes, but that's been resolved. Look, I understand what you're saying and...

**Worthy:** Yeah, it was resolved all right, but I have the feeling that even though I gave in to your ideas because you're the boss, you know how I feel. Frank, it isn't right to hold that against me!

**Harlow:** I haven't been holding anything against you, and I wasn't aware that you gave in because I'm the boss. You agreed that the indirect concept would work better... or did you really agree?

**Worthy:** Yeah, OK, I agreed. So you were right. Who am I to argue with authority? Anyhow, are you going to listen to what I have to say about the way I'm being paid? I mean, I know Harry Crother got a raise just recently...

**Harlow:** Manny, we don't have time to go into this situation in depth right now. Why don't you arrange to spend an hour or so with me next Tuesday morning to discuss your personal progress and the question you've raised about your ideas being pushed aside. We can bring up the money thing after we have those items resolved.

### ANALYSIS: THERE'S A SCARED CHILD PROTESTING
#### Seeking a Pay Raise

**Script Theme:** "You can't win."

**Tapes:** Parent—"Father knows best." "You're stupid."
Child —"I'll hide my real feelings."

**Key Crossed Transaction:**

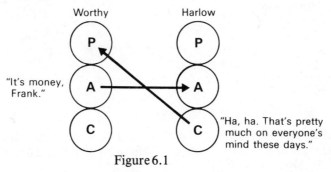

Figure 6.1

**Ulterior Message:** "You're out to get me."

**Basic Life Position:** "I'm not-OK—you're OK."

**Game:** *Wooden Leg*

**Role:** Victim ("...but I have the feeling that even though I gave in to your ideas because you're the boss...")

Emanuel believes the world is against him, and his Parent selects evidence to prove that to his Child. His Adult is not aware of this behavior even though it is going on right inside his head. His script drags people in to play parts that fit with its basic theme, which makes him a loser. He deals with reality but goes for the reality that fits his script, rather than letting the facts speak for themselves and form their own pattern. All this makes life predictable for his Child, even though the outcome is negative. The world in his view is predictably against him.

He does get on an Adult-Adult level with Frank when he comes out straight with the request for a raise.

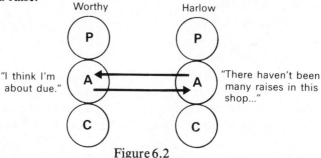

Figure 6.2

But the transaction does not remain complementary for long. Emanuel's Parent gets hooked when it looks as though his Child will not get the goodies he wants. The Parent is defensive, as if saying "I'll take care of them for ya." His defense is an attack on whatever is regarded as an enemy of the Child.

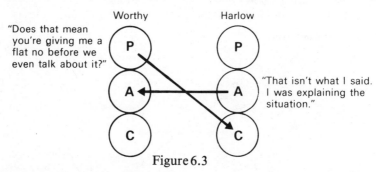

Figure 6.3

Frank is vainly looking for Manny's lost Adult, which is no longer activated. The energy lodged in Manny's Parent quickly slips to his Child, and what he was dumping out suddenly becomes dumped in.

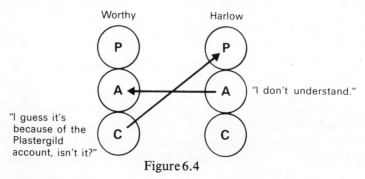

Figure 6.4

His Parent starts berating his Child for being so incompetent and having made such terrible mistakes. Manny is now in his scared Child. His Parent is calling him stupid.

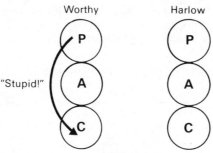

Figure 6.5

There must be some reason for his not getting a raise. Either it is Frank's fault or it is his own. Manny is more likely to blame himself. He internalizes his anger, as he was taught to do when he was a child. So he burns inside.

As a child he had to go along with what his parents said, like it or not, and it was usually not. But children in his family were not allowed to say what they really felt. They had to cover up negative feelings with more acceptable ones—which were really not their own. The parents taught them to be plastic and phoney rather than genuine and honest. Consequently Manny could never be quite sure what his feelings really were. He puts Daddy's face on Frank to fit his script so he can play his Victim role. He does not really listen to Frank, who is obviously confused by this scripty behavior.

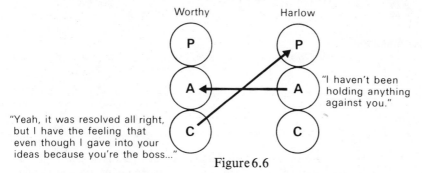

Figure 6.6

And since he pays so little real attention to the here and now, whatever real help he might get from Frank is lost.

## Awareness Format

Revise the script by writing your own version of this dialogue, which has ended so badly. Use the Awareness Format to do it, and then compare your version with ours. A sample for the Awareness Format is provided in the appendix.

### I. Tapes
Change Manny's Child tape ("I'll hide my real feelings.") into an Adult statement.

Adult: _____

_____

Change Manny's Parent tape ("Father knows best." "You're stupid.") into an Adult statement.

Adult: _____

_____

### II. Key Crossed Transaction
Change the crossed transaction (see Fig. 6.1) to make it complementary.

Manny: _____

_____

Frank: _____

_____

### III. Ulterior Message
Change Manny's Ulterior Message ("You're out to get me.") into an Adult statement.
Adult: _____

_____

### IV. Role
Change what Manny said in his Victim role to an Adult statement.
Victim: "...but I have the feeling that even though I gave in to your ideas because you're the boss..."
Adult: _____

_____

_____

_____

## V. Style

On a scale from 1 to 10 grade the applicability of each criterion from Manny's point of view. (See the introduction to this book for a detailed explanation of the criteria.)

Grade
1 to 10

A. A Developmental style may be effective:

   1. The Adult is available in the other person. _____

   2. A joint decision is important. _____

   3. An impasse has been reached and a new approach is desired. _____

   4. There is time for study and discussion. _____

B. A Controlling style may be effective:

   1. The chief priority is to get the task done as soon as possible. _____

   2. You intend to direct the project in your own way. _____

   3. Ready assent is forthcoming from the other person's Child. _____

   4. Negotiation is futile, and you control all the alternatives. _____

C. A Relinquishing style may be effective:

   1. The other person has relevant information which you do not possess. _____

   2. The other person's Child is upset and needs your Nurturing Parent. _____

   3. Development of the other person's autonomy is the most important objective. _____

   4. The other person is autonomous, yet a caring relationship still exists. _____

D. A Defensive style may be effective:

   1. Your Child is confused or frustrated. _____

   2. Participation is against the moral standards of your Parent. _____

   3. Your support is not required. _____

   4. You are aware that games are being played. _____

Fill in the criteria score chart below according to the numbers indicated for each style. Use the criteria score chart to select a transactional style which is designed to effectively achieve Manny's Desired Result.

Criteria Score Chart

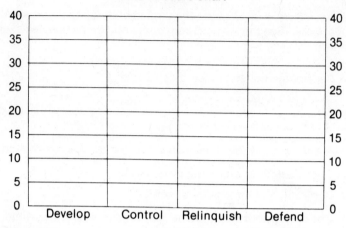

If another style is graded close to the highest one on your chart, you may want to incorporate that in your approach. Both may be appropriate at different times in the dialogue or discussion.

*Strategy*

1. What style is indicated for the Improved Dialogue?  _____

_____

2. Make some notes on how Manny's strategy might be improved, using the style indicated.

_____

_____

_____

_____

_____

_____

_____

_____

_____

_____

---

---

---

---

Now read the Improved Dialogue and compare it with what you have written in Sections I through V.

## THE IMPROVED DIALOGUE
### Seeking a Pay Raise

Transactional Analysis, in this instance as in any other, cannot and will not perform miracles of character change. Manny's background as a child, extrapolated in our analysis from the original dialogue, will not simply fade away into oblivion. It will exist to haunt Manny in anything he does for the rest of his life. Being Transactionally Aware can help him to control that terrified Child and cool the hotblooded Parent. Each of them will, from time to time, assert itself and it is Manny's Transactional Awareness that should make it possible for him to put them back into the dormant subconscious for as long as possible... and to overcome, by OK dialogue coming from his Adult, the damage they might do to a transaction. Like this...

Worthy is at the open door of Harlow's office.

**Worthy:** Say, Frank, can I talk to you for a couple of minutes?

**Harlow:** Sure, come in... I've got about twenty minutes before a policy meeting upstairs...

**Worthy:** Swell. (*Goes into the office*) Mind if I close the door? This is personal.

**Harlow:** Go ahead. Sit down and tell me what's on your mind.

**Worthy:** Thanks. It's money, Frank.

**Harlow:** (*Laugh*) That's pretty much on everyone's mind nowadays, isn't it?

**Worthy:** Listen, it's no laughing matter, Frank, I'm pretty serious about this.

**Harlow:** OK, OK, Manny, I didn't mean for it to sound that way.

**Worthy:** Look, I do a pretty good job around here, right?

**Harlow:** I have no major complaints.

**Worthy:** Well, I haven't had a raise in about a year. I think I'm about due, it's just as simple as that, Frank.

**Harlow:** Put on that basis, Manny, let me be straight with you... There haven't been many raises in this shop for the past 12-14 months. You know what business has been like.

**Worthy:** Say does that mean—that is... you aren't closing the door on talking about the possibility are you, Frank? I mean, I can appreciate that what you're saying is true.

**Harlow:** I'm glad you do understand that the company hasn't liked the idea of frozen salaries for this long and of course the door isn't closed. Far from it.

**Worthy:** Listen, I know we had a little run-in on the Plastergild account...

**Harlow:** Well...

**Worthy:** It's my job to put up a struggle for the ideas I present, and it took a while to convince me that the indirect concept was best.

**Harlow:** Were you convinced or did you just back off?

**Worthy:** I hate to admit it, but I was convinced. I just want to be sure that there isn't something about that situation that might affect the possibility of my getting a raise.

**Harlow:** Not at all.

**Worthy:** Fine... Look, I'm not asking for the world. Just enough to even me up with the cost of living. You know what's happened.

**Harlow:** I do, Manny. We're pushing for some efficiencies in our placement of outside work, and I'm going to ask you to spend some time with me working on it later this week. I think we can have some success there. In addition, there's a good chance that the Plastergild people will increase their budget. Between those two events, we could find ouselves in a somewhat better cash flow position. As part of our discussion of outside work savings, let's include the need to get you more money... I think it can be worked out. How about Wednesday... say, 4 PM?

**Worthy:** Fine. And thanks.

Dear reader, please don't leave this chapter with a sense of euphoria. Worthy's change in approach would be likely to have more salutary results than his original hysteria... but it is not guaranteed. What you have read here is a rather optimistic possibility in this transaction. Reality might very well have said that Worthy just isn't worth more money for the work he can do, or that the company actually is on the verge of bankruptcy. Barring those possibilities, however, a TA approach should have results very similar to those indicated herein.

## Awareness Format Applied to Your Own Situation

### I. Background
Describe briefly a situation in which you have had a responsible part and are not satisfied with the results:

_____

_____

_____

### II. Desired Result
What was your Desired Result? _____

_____

### III. Key Crossed Transaction
In that situation identify a key crossed transaction in which the response came from the Parent or the Child in the other person.

What you said: _____

_____

The response: _____

_____

Diagram your crossed transaction:

### IV. Tapes
Imagine yourself as you were when you were a very young child and think of an experience which is similar to the one you have just described. Be aware of the people who appear in your mind's eye, what you felt and what you were trying to say to them.

In the recent situation which you have just described, what appears to be the Child tape influencing your behavior from that old scene in your past?

Child tape: _____

_____

Change your Child tape into an Adult statement:

Adult: _____

_____

What appears to be your Parent tape? If you need to, go back to the memory you just retrieved for an awareness of that tape.

Parent tape: _____

_____

Change your Parent tape into an Adult statement:

Adult: _____

_____

## V. Ulterior Message
What Ulterior Message did you send to the other person? You can spot your Ulterior Message by examining your Parent and Child tapes to see how they exerted a negative influence on your transactional style in that situation.

Your Ulterior Message: _____

_____

## VI. Basic Life Position
Check out your feelings in that situation. What Basic Life Position do they seem to indicate?

Check one:   ☐ I'm not-OK—you're OK.
             ☐ I'm not-OK—you're not-OK.
             ☐ I'm OK—you're not-OK.
             ☐ I'm OK—you're OK.

What is the feeling? _____

## VII. Game Awareness
Now you can see how the parts of your game fall into place. Write here your Desired Result (see II above).

_____

Write here your Ulterior Message (see V above).

_____

Write here the response you got in the crossed transaction (see III above).

_____

Write here your Basic Life Position in that situation (see VI above) and the feeling that goes with it.

Basic Life Position:_____

Feeling: _____

What game seems to be indicated here?

Name: _____

To get out of that game, change your Ulterior Message in that game into an Adult statement.

Adult: _____

_____

## VIII. Role

What role were you playing in that game? Check one:

☐ Persecutor    ☐ Victim    ☐ Rescuer

Describe what you said or did to play that role.

_____

_____

Change that to an Adult behavior or statement:

Adult: _____

_____

## IX. Style

On a scale from 1 to 10 grade the applicability of each criterion from your point of view. (See the introduction to this book for a detailed explanation of the criteria.)

Grade
1 to 10

A. A Developmental style may be effective:

1. The Adult is available in the other person.        _____

2. A joint decision is important.        _____

3. An impasse has been reached and a new approach is desired.        _____

4. There is time for study and discussion.        _____

B. A Controlling style may be effective:

1. The chief priority is to get the task done as soon as possible. _____

2. You intend to direct the project in your own way. _____

3. Ready assent is forthcoming from the other person's Child. _____

4. Negotiation is futile, and you control all the alternatives. _____

C. A Relinquishing style may be effective:

1. The other person has relevant information which you do not possess. _____

2. The other person's Child is upset and needs your Nurturing Parent. _____

3. Development of the other person's autonomy is the most important objective. _____

4. The other person is autonomous, yet a caring relationship still exists. _____

D. A Defensive style may be effective:

1. Your Child is confused or frustrated. _____

2. Participation is against the moral standards of your Parent. _____

3. Your support is not required. _____

4. You are aware that games are being played. _____

Fill in the criteria score chart below, Use the criteria score chart to develop a transactional strategy that will effectively attain your Desired Result.

Criteria Score Chart

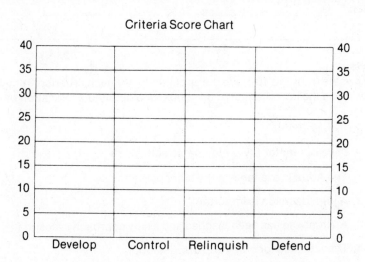

If some other style appears to be close to another one on your chart, you may want to incorporate that in your approach. Both may be appropriate at different times in the dialogue or discussion.

*Strategy*

1. What style is indicated for your Improved Dialogue?

_____

2. Look over carefully what you have written in Sections I-IX and use it to help yourself decide how to implement that style. Then make some notes on what you will do:

_____

_____

_____

_____

_____

_____

_____

_____

_____

_____

_____

3. When will you do it? _____

_____

# CHAPTER SEVEN

# It is a sad commentary...

**Subject:** Refusing a pay raise
**Initiator:** Employee
**Point of View:** Employer
**Desired Result:**Acceptance of situation by employee without loss of morale
**Employee:** Kenneth Seeker     **Employer (immediate superior):** Hudson Stone

Kenneth Seeker is a managing editor for the Stone Publishing Company. Hudson Stone, the president and publisher, is a scion of the family that founded the company and maintains personal control. His relationship with his "executive family" is close and direct. Seeker has been in his office discussing the slant of an issue of one of their trade magazines. That subject has been covered when Seeker springs a bit of surprise.

**Seeker:** Mr. Stone, would I be out of line if I spoke very directly?

**Stone:** Not at all... We've never beaten around the bush in this office, Kenneth.

**Seeker:** Well, I think I'm entitled to a raise in pay. After all, I've taken on an extra publication, which means my duties have expanded.

**Stone:** Well, now, did you feel that the extra work put too much of a load on your shoulders?

**Seeker:** No, I can handle it all right. But it seems to me that I'm saving the company a good bit of money by...

**Stone:** Kenneth, you know the second book you're working on has been a money-loser for months.

**Seeker:** Sure, but your costs to put it out stay the same... I think I can turn around the profit-loss picture on it, but...

**Stone:** That's good to hear. Don't you think, then, it would make sense to discuss your salary after you've shown me some results on that book?

**Seeker:** Mr. Stone, I sort of felt that I'd proven my ability and that you had faith in my ability when you put me in charge of the extra project. I mean, my salary hasn't changed in about six months and I think...

**Stone:** I'm sorry, Kenneth, but it isn't possible to consider pay increases at this time. It is a sad commentary if my faith in your ability has to be measured by the amount of added money I hand you each time I ask you to handle a special task—now, wouldn't you agree, Kenneth?

**Seeker:** Well, I'm not putting a hard price on...

**Stone:** Good. I'm glad you see it my way. When I feel that we can discuss a raise on the basis of results with the second book, I'll certainly bring it up again. Was there anything else you wanted to discuss?

**Seeker:** I guess that's it. I'll tell my family our vacation this year will have to be at home... By the way, I'll be taking it earlier than I had originally intended...

## ANALYSIS: SELFLESS DEVOTION TO SERVICE
### Refusing a Pay Raise

**Script Theme:** "Hard work, like virtue, is its own reward."

**Tapes:** Parent—"Be like your father; keep up our proud tradition."

Child—"Gee, Dad, you're wonderful."

**Key Crossed Transaction:**

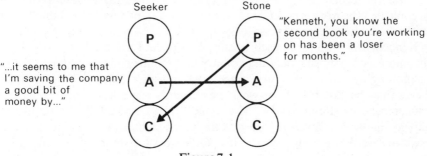

Figure 7.1

**Ulterior Message:** "You could have done it bigger and better."

**Basic Life Position:** "I'm OK—you're not-OK."

**Game:** *Workaholic*

**Role:** Persecutor ("It's sad commentary if my faith in your ability has to be measured by the amount of added money I hand you...")


Hudson Stone has not questioned or critically examined his Parent ego state. He has had no need to. It all works fine—for him. Why question a good thing? His Child ego state remains secure, basking in the splendor of the success which the Parent has consistently produced.

For Hudson Stone, as it probably had been for his family, the slogan was "Hard work never hurt anyone." We can assume that it was always clear to him that their wealth was a sacred trust which called for the highest level of devoted service and responsibility to the community.

The wealth of the Stones resides mainly in the company itself, however, as a kind of trust which they are given the responsibility to maintain. Their devoted service provides an example of edification and enlightenment to the community. Selfish personal use of the money would be severely frowned upon by the great Stone visage in the ancestral portraits which doubtless appear throughout the family estate.

On the other hand, it is evident that Stone would not have maintained his position in the company if he were not an intelligent, hard-headed businessman, as well. As such, he harbors a benign attitude toward Kenneth Seeker, whom he does not consciously intend to put down. Presumably, he would prefer that he could refuse the pay raise for sound business reasons and have it graciously and rationally accepted in this situation. However, the reality gets lost in the games that take over the action in accord with their scripts.

Kenneth Seeker, though of a humbler class, was brought up with a script similar to that of the eminent Hudson. These very Parent tapes were what attracted him to the Stone Publishing Company in the first place. It was like moving into the big house on the hill, even though it was only into the servants' quarters. Perhaps his parents told him, "Ken, you can play when the work is done." However, the ulterior message in that could be "the work is never done." If so, little Ken had never read that fine print, but it's there in the Parent message.

Kenneth sets it up for himself because his appeal for a raise in pay is that he is doing more work and so would like to have more money and more fun. That hooks him thoroughly into the big steel trap in Mr. Stone's mind. Mr. Stone's Parent believes that the just reward of work well done is more work, or in their elegant phrase, more opportunity to serve. Mr. Stone's Parent is so solidly identified with the company that Ken's Child ego state doesn't have a chance. And Mr. Stone's Child is there to please that Parent. Clearly, his Adult would operate differently, if it were indeed operating in this situation.

As the dialogue begins, Stone's Parent is immediately suspicious of Seeker's request for more pay. After all, doesn't all that run contrary to his ideals of selfless devotion to the splendid ideal of service? Even though he may feel somewhat critical of his subordinate, Stone uses his paternalistic Nurturing Parent to respond, and so crosses the transaction:

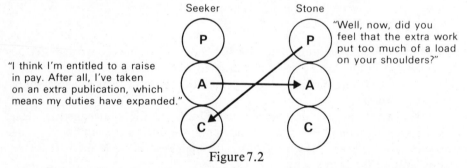

Figure 7.2

Unfortunately, Stone does not respond to the information that is being presented to him. Rather, Stone expects compliance from Kenneth's Child. Instead, he gets more Adult information. His Parent doesn't want information, however, so its critical side emerges to deal with what appears to be an obstinate boy (Fig. 7.3). Here the game gets underway. Stone's Parent is not interested in rewards or advancement to Seeker, and that interferes with his Adult ability to be rational.

The Ulterior Message in Mr. Stone's *Workaholic* game is "you could have done it bigger and better." It is like the addictive aspect of alcohol. There is no joy in it, only further compulsion. The choices are long since past and only the habit controls the

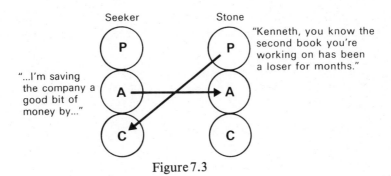

Figure 7.3

behavior. When he holds out for discussing Seeker's salary after they've "seen some results," that is rational enough, but he does not adequately clarify his position. How does Seeker know that Stone will not find another excuse at that time, find more fault, and expect another project to be undertaken?

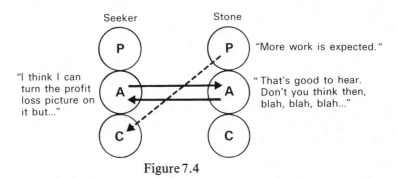

Figure 7.4

Stone's game of *Workaholic* reaffirms his Parent Basic Life Position that subordinates are lazy and greedy, i. e., "I'm OK—you're not-OK." At best, subordinates can only be tolerated and shown examples of selfless devotion to the ideal of service. To accomplish this, his Parent drives him as hard as it does others. His game provides him with the means of furthering his script and collecting gold stamps. He may even cash in his gold stamps for a trip to Europe once in five years, a reward to which he is "entitled" after having "served so long, so hard and so well."

If his Adult were working in this situation he would not engage in moralisms about his "faith in the ability of his employee..." Rather, he would give specifics about why it is not possible to consider the pay increase at this time, and that information, addressed to Seeker's Adult, could provoke a response at the Adult level instead of the obvious breakdown in communications. Stone has simply not given enough facts and is avoiding the real problem by giving out Parent moralisms instead.

Kenneth's script prevents him from reading the reality of the situation also. He has been taught to wait, without realizing that it is forever. He aims for what he believes to be the real options with his Adult, not realizing that his Child has already acquiesced to an impossible situation. Stone's Adult is unavailable and all Kenneth gets is the great Stone face.

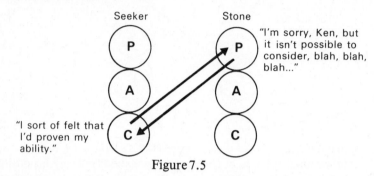

Figure 7.5

The script line is brought out in the august statement, "It is a sad commentary if my faith in your ability has to be measured by the amount of added money I hand you each time I ask you to handle a specific task." The Stone Parent is in control. The probability of its changing is as high as that of moving Mt. Everest. How could this Parent tolerate the debasement of such a noble tradition by allowing service to the cause to be mentioned in the same breath with cash? As with all rhetorical Parent questions, no answer is expected.

Stone's Parent wants to be very sure that no initiative is granted to the lowly Kenneth. His Adult knows he needs him to produce and to feel good about it. If you were Stone, and you really wanted morale for Kenneth, and yet could not increase his pay, what would you do instead?

## Awareness Format

Revise the script by writing your own version of this dialogue, which has ended so badly. Use the Awareness Format to do it, and then compare your version with ours. A sample for the Awareness Format is provided in the appendix.

### I. Tapes
Change Stone's Child tape ("Gee, Dad, you're wonderful.") into an Adult statement.

Adult: _____

_____

Change Stone's Parent tape ("Be like your father; keep up our proud tradition.") into an Adult statement.

Adult: _____

_____

## II. Key Crossed Transaction
Change the crossed transaction (see Fig. 7.1) to make it complementary.

Adult: _____

_____

## III. Ulterior Message
Change Stone's Ulterior Message ("You could have done it bigger and better.") into an Adult statement.

Adult: _____

_____

## IV. Role
Change what Stone said in his Persecutor role to an Adult statement.

Persecutor: "It's a sad commentary if my faith in your ability has to be measured by the amount of added money I hand you..."

Adult: _____

_____

## V. Style
On a scale from 1 to 10 grade the applicability of each criterion from Stone's point of view. (See the introduction to this book for a detailed explanation of the criteria.)

Grade 1 to 10

A. A Developmental style may be effective:

  1. The adult is available in the other person. _____

  2. A joint decision is important. _____

  3. An impasse has been reached and a new approach is desired. _____

  4. There is time for study and discussion. _____

B. A Controlling style may be effective:

  1. The chief priority is to get the task done as soon as possible. _____

  2. You intend to direct the project in your own way. _____

  3. Ready assent is forthcoming from the other person's Child. _____

  4. Negotiation is futile, and you control all the alternatives. _____

C. A Relinquishing style may be effective:

  1. The other person has relevant information which you do not possess. _____

  2. The other person's Child is upset and needs your Nurturing Parent. _____

3. Development of the other person's autonomy is the most important objective. _____

4. The other person is autonomous, yet a caring relationship still exists. _____

D. A Defensive style may be effective:

1. Your Child is confused or frustrated. _____

2. Participation is against the moral standards of your Parent. _____

3. Your support is not required. _____

4. You are aware that games are being played. _____

Fill in the criteria score chart below according to the numbers indicated for each style. Use the criteria score chart to select a transactional style which is designed to effectively achieve Stone's Desired Result.

Criteria Score Chart

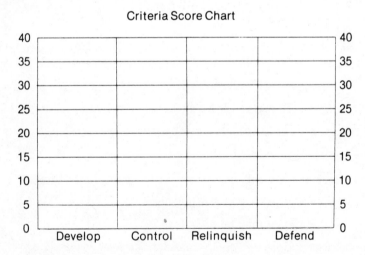

If another style is graded close to the highest one on your chart, you may want to incorporate that in your approach. Both may be appropriate at different times in the dialogue or discussion.

*Strategy*

1. What style is indicated for the Improved Dialogue? _____

_____

2. Make some notes on how Stone's strategy might be improved, using the style indicated.

_____

_____

_____

_____

_____

_____

_____

_____

_____

_____

_____

_____

Now read the Improved Dialogue and compare it with what you have written in Sections I through V.

## THE IMPROVED DIALOGUE
### Refusing a Pay Raise

Hudson Stone, being fully aware of his own transactional attitudes as our scenario reopens, has what amounts to a marvelous opportunity. The point here being that in order to attain the results desired from a given transaction, it is by no means necessary to maintain a totally Adult approach. Nor is it always the most useful technique to reach only the transactional partner's Adult throughout the dialogue. In order to maintain Kenneth Seeker's good will and enthusiasm for his job while refusing a raise, it is almost essential that Kenneth's Child be stroked with a showering of nonfinancial gold stamps while the Seeker Adult is being, quite simply, stalled. There is little doubt that the desire, indeed the need, for a raise in pay is not something that an employer can permanently obliterate in one masterful verbal coup. The best result of this transaction obviously is a maintenance of Seeker's enthusiasm and a delay in his money demands.

**Seeker:** Mr. Stone, would I be out of line if I spoke very directly?

**Stone:** Not at all... We've never beaten around the bush in this office, Kenneth.

**Seeker:** Well, I think I'm entitled to a raise in pay. After all, I've taken on an extra publication, which means my duties have expanded...

**Stone:** Kenneth, I asked you to take on that other book because I felt and I still feel that you're the man who can turn it around.

**Seeker:** Well...I do appreciate your confidence, Mr. Stone. But it seems to me that you'd have to hire another man and that would have cost...

**Stone:** Kenneth, please. We're in that project together. The fact is, and you're familiar enough with the business to understand this, we would simply have killed the second publication if we had to invest more money in personnel for it.

**Seeker:** Oh, sure, I can see that. But still, if you think about it, my salary hasn't changed in about six months and I feel as if the effort I'm putting out...

**Stone:** No argument. You are doing a yeoman job on your basic assignment as well as the second book. What's happening, Kenneth, is that we're both investing in that new project. You're investing a good deal of additional effort, the company's putting up substantial risk capital. Can you accept that?

**Seeker:** Yes... but...

**Stone:** Before you protest, let me offer a solid compromise. By no means a rejection, although it means that you won't get that raise right now. First, I need your considered opinion. Do you feel that the second book can show a profit in a reasonable time?

**Seeker:** Yes. You haven't held back on editiorial expenditures or quality production. Yes, I can do it.

**Stone:** That's what I thought you'd say, Kenneth. My confidence isn't misplaced! Very well then, would you say that in two months we can pretty well see if those results will come to pass?

**Seeker:** Yes, I think so.

**Stone:** Good. Now, we both understand that despite your best efforts, it might not work out. Therefore, I will not say to you that your raise depends on success with the second book... It merely means that for now, I'm asking you to help us put capital into the quality of that book. After two months—or sooner, if we get encouraging results—we'll talk about a raise in very positive terms.

**Seeker:** Well, I've got confidence in that book, but you're right, the conditions of the market could conceivably stop us. If you have to kill it, though...

**Stone:** Kenneth, if *we* decide to kill it—I wouldn't make the judgment without taking your view into full consideration—it will mean that the financial burden will have been lifted to an extent and your raise will still be possible. (*Laugh*) Truthfully, though, I meant what I said when I told you we are in that enterprise together—and your raise could be somewhat more substantial if we make a go of the book!

**Seeker:** (*Entering into the spirit*) Fair enough! Be ready to talk about a good sized raise in two months... or less!

## Awareness Format Applied to Your Own Situation

### I. Background
Describe briefly a situation in which you have had a responsible part and are not satisfied with the results:

_____

_____

_____

### II. Desired Result
What was your Desired Result? _____

_____

### III. Key Crossed Transaction
In that situation identify a key crossed transaction in which the response came from the Parent or the Child in the other person.

What you said: _____

_____

The response: _____

_____

Diagram your crossed transaction:

### IV. Tapes
Imagine yourself as you were when you were a very young child and think of an experience which is similar to the one you have just described. Be aware of the people who appear in your mind's eye, what you felt and what you were trying to say to them.

In the recent situation which you have just described, what appears to be the Child tape influencing your behavior from that old scene in your past?

Child tape: _____

_____

Change your Child tape into an Adult statement:

Adult: _____

_____

What appears to be your Parent tape? If you need to, go back to the memory you just retrieved for an awareness of that tape.

Parent tape: _____

_____

Change your Parent tape into an Adult statement:

Adult: _____

_____

## V. Ulterior Message
What Ulterior Message did you send to the other person? You can spot your Ulterior Message by examining your Parent and Child tapes to see how they exerted a negative influence on your transactional style in that situation.

Your Ulterior Message: _____

_____

## VI. Basic Life Position
Check out your feelings in that situation. What Basic Life Position do they seem to indicate?

Check one:  ☐ I'm not-OK—you're OK.
☐ I'm not-OK—you're not-OK.
☐ I'm OK—you're not-OK.
☐ I'm OK—you're OK.

What is the feeling? _____

## VII. Game Awareness
Now you can see how the parts of your game fall into place. Write here your Desired Result (see II above).

_____

Write here your Ulterior Message (see V above).

_____

Write here the response you got in the crossed transaction (see III above).

_____

Write here your Basic Life Position in that situation (see VI above) and the feeling that goes with it.

Basic Life Position: _____

Feeling: _____

What game seems to be indicated here?

Name: _____

To get out of that game, change your Ulterior Message in that game into an Adult statement.

Adult: _____

_____

## VIII. Role

What role were you playing in that game? Check one:

☐ Persecutor  ☐ Victim  ☐ Rescuer

Describe what you said or did to play that role.

_____

_____

Change that to an Adult behavior or statement:

Adult: _____

_____

## IX. Style

On a scale from 1 to 10 grade the applicability of each criterion from your point of view. (See the introduction to this book for a detailed explanation of the criteria.)

Grade
1 to 10

A. A Developmental style may be effective:

1. The Adult is available in the other person.          _____

2. A joint decision is important.          _____

3. An impasse has been reached and a new approach is desired.          _____

4. There is time for study and discussion.          _____

B. A Controlling style may be effective:

   1. The chief priority is to get the task done as soon as possible. _____

   2. You intend to direct the project in your own way. _____

   3. Ready assent is forthcoming from the other person's Child. _____

   4. Negotiation is futile, and you control all the alternatives. _____

C. A Relinquishing style may be effective:

   1. The other person has relevant information which you do not possess. _____

   2. The other person's Child is upset and needs your Nurturing Parent. _____

   3. Development of the other person's autonomy is the most important objective. _____

   4. The other person is autonomous, yet a caring relationship still exists. _____

D. A Defensive style may be effective:

   1. Your Child is confused or frustrated. _____

   2. Participation is against the moral standards of your Parent. _____

   3. Your support is not required. _____

   4. You are aware that games are being played. _____

Fill in the criteria score chart below, Use the criteria score chart to develop a transactional strategy that will effectively attain your Desired Result.

Criteria Score Chart

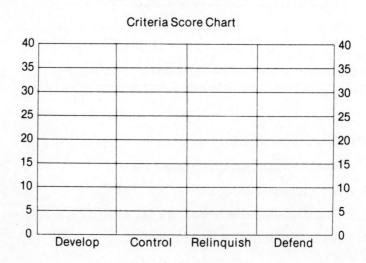

If some other style appears to be close to another one on your chart, you may want to incorporate that in your approach. Both may be appropriate at different times in the dialogue or discussion.

*Strategy*

1. What style is indicated for your Improved Dialogue?

_____

2. Look over carefully what you have written in Sections I-IX and use it to help yourself decide how to implement that style. Then make some notes on what you will do:

_____
_____
_____
_____
_____
_____
_____
_____
_____
_____

3. When will you do it? _____

_____

# CHAPTER EIGHT

# Boy, you really do have surprises for me!

**Subject:** Employee relocation with minor promotion
**Initiator:** Employer
**Point of View:** Employer
**Desired Result:** Acceptance of relocation without loss of morale
**Employer:** John Major, National Sales Manager    **Employee:** Andrew Fieldman

Andrew Fieldman has been a successful sales representative for the Sweetooth Candy Co. for several years, working in the upper New York State territory. An account manager's position has opened up in Duluth and John Major wants Fieldman to take the job. It's a bit more responsibility since he'll call on select accounts and there is a salary increase. After appropriate greetings, Fieldman is seated opposite Major in Major's office.

**Major:** How was the flight from Albany, Andy?

**Fieldman:** Kinda bumpy. I never liked flying anyway... It's a lucky thing, I guess, that my territory can be handled by a guy with a car... (*Laughs*)

**Major:** (*Joins in laughter*) Yeah, I suppose so. Andy, I don't want to keep you in suspense. Your division manager told you that I wanted to see you to talk about a promotion.

**Fieldman:** He did, and I appreciate it.

**Major:** Well, the job I want you to take over is as account manager.

**Fieldman:** Account manager? Oh, well, listen, terrific!... (*Laugh*) ... You know, when Harry talked to me I sort of got the impression he was moving up and that...

**Major:** No, Andy, the division manager's job isn't open. That doesn't mean that you won't some day be stepping into that position. Anyway, I've got a lot of confidence in you and I wouldn't ask you to take over this set of accounts if I didn't think you could handle the responsibility.

**Fieldman:** Thanks, John, I appreciate that. You'd think that Harry wouldn't have kept me hanging for two weeks till I talked to you, though... (*Nervous laugh*)... It doesn't matter, though. Say, is Merv moving on or something? How long has he been account manager in New York State?

**Major:** Oh, Merv isn't moving. It isn't New York State that we're talking about, Andy. It's Duluth.

**Fieldman:** Where?

**Major:** Duluth. Now remember, we pay all moving expenses, help you find a new house—the whole ball of wax... and there's a $4000 increase in it for you.

**Fieldman:** Uh, how soon do I have to make this move?

**Major:** We'd like you to take over out there right away... I can arrange for your New York territory to be covered starting a week from today...

**Fieldman:** Boy, you really do have some surprises for me, don't you? . . . Honestly, John, it's sort of tough. . . My family hasn't ever lived anywhere but Albany. . .

**Major:** Oh, they'll love it in Duluth, great schools, good people out there. . .

**Fieldman:** And there's my house. . .

**Major:** We'll make sure you don't get hurt on it, Andy.

**Fieldman:** My daughter is going to graduate from high school next year. . . You know, I could face a family rebellion on this. . .

**Major:** Just explain the facts of life to 'em, Andy. . . I mean, what's more important—sticking in a neighborhood, or dad's job that puts goodies in their mouths? You know what I mean? Just explain it and make your position clear. . .

**Fieldman:** Just what *is* my position, John? I mean, I'm not sure I could fit in out there. . .

**Major:** Andy, this is the result of a lot of discussion at top management level, and it's been decided that Duluth is a natural spot for you. . . We didn't make this decision suddenly, I can tell you. . .

**Fieldman:** Been discussing it here at the home office for some time, huh?

**Major:** Yeah.

**Fieldman:** And now you made up your minds and you want me to get out there next week, right?

**Major:** Right. We. . . well, it reflects our feelings about your ability. . .

**Fieldman:** And you've made arrangements to cover my New York territory?

**Major:** Right. Harry will show the new guy the ropes.

**Fieldman:** Got it all worked out. I'm kinda sorry that in all this planning and discussion nobody thought of talking to me. . .

**Major:** Well, I wanted to be sure I had the advancement to offer you before I got your expectations up, you know?

**Fieldman:** Thanks. Listen, I'm flying home tonight and I'll talk to my family about this.

**Major:** And then you'll be ready to take over out there.

**Fieldman:** I'll call you tomorrow from home and talk about it, John. I'm not ready right now to say anything positive. . . 'Bye. . . I want to catch an earlier plane home.

### ANALYSIS: A ONE-WAY STREET
#### Employee Relocation with Minor Promotion

**Script Theme:** "Be sure you're right."

**Tapes:** Parent—"Take care of your boys."
  Child—"I'll do whatever you say." "My feelings don't count."

**Key Crossed Transaction:**

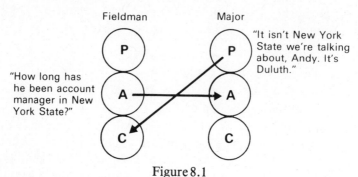

Fieldman     Major

"How long has he been account manager in New York State?"

"It isn't New York State we're talking about, Andy. It's Duluth."

Figure 8.1

**Ulterior Message:** "We've got you by the balls."

**Basic Life Position:** "I'm OK—you're not-OK."

**Games:** *Corner, I'm Only Trying to Help You*

**Role:** Persecutor/Rescuer ("Oh, they'll love it in Duluth, great schools, good people out there...")

John Major's Parent ego state is cautious, and serious about being right. It follows Abraham Lincoln's admonition. "Be sure you're right, then go ahead." Negotiation does not characterize this attitude. Rather, it is a one-way street, which is taken *after* all the options have been considered. In John's script this is perfectly acceptable behavior. Anything else, in fact, would be considered irresponsible and even frivolous. Things are done slowly, carefully and well, according to that script; and since they are, it is only appropriate that others fit in with what has been so conscientiously put together. Every consideration is given to the needs of those being served with due regard for their individual proclivities. But at the same time a realistic view is held of major priorities.

All this works fine except that, as Andrew Fieldman points out, "in all this planning and discussion nobody thought of talking to me..."

Certainly John Major is benign. Even when he has to be forceful, it is with the best interests of his employee in mind, as when he says, "What's more important—sticking in a neighborhood, or dad's job that puts goodies in their mouths?" He even gives advice on how to speak to the children.

The Desired Result is lost because not only does Andrew not accept the offer, but clearly his morale is seriously threatened. He has no commitment to a decision which has been made for him, and to which he has not been allowed to contribute. John Major's method of dealing with his employee's resistance is to seek to control him further. Naturally, the resistance escalates.

As the dialogue begins, it is clear that Andrew is in his Child ego state. His expectations are very high—higher than the situation calls for, and so he is bound to feel the letdown.

Gently, but firmly, John's Parent strokes Andrew's Child.

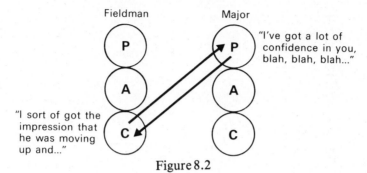

Figure 8.2

Unfortunately, Andrew's Adult is not functioning. If it were, perhaps he could accept the facts more readily, even as he feels the disappointment in his Child. However, John does not see that the *decision to accept* the change cannot be made for Andrew. In other words, he needs his employee's Adult for the decision to be effective, because it is the Adult which is the change agent of the personality. It is the frustration of all parents, that they cannot give their children the Adult. That is the responsibility of the children. John's Parent is now facing that frustration in dealing with Andrew's Child. To bring about his Desired Result he needs to address that part of his employee's personality which can accept new information rationally, rather than emotionally. But the Good Parent walks right into the trap of trying too hard to take care of the Child—and as a result has on his hands only a child. His rescuing attempts only perpetuate his Victim's inadequacy. Andrew's problem is compounded by the fact that he has spent a long time waiting—two weeks—and that's a long time to wait for Christmas.

Andrew's Adult does not spark and splutter enough to seek to get information. It gets too contaminated by the heavy disappointment in his Child, which is covered up with a nervous laugh. All this lead to a crossed transaction which ends up in hooking his Parent in the end.

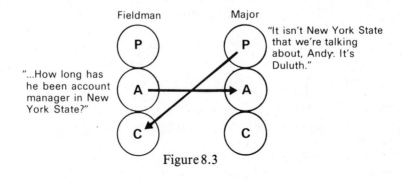

Figure 8.3

John's Parent is watching out for Andrew, but in the phrase, "...that we're talking about," the "we" does not refer just to Andy and John. The pronoun "we" indicates a collective decision, which he is simply presenting. There are benefits, which he points out—moving expenses, help with a new house, an increase in pay. But it's a foregone conclusion that he is talking about, and in no way is it a discussion to explore options.

All of Andrew's protests are met with reasonable, caring directives. Since these protests are coming mainly from his Parent, the two men are talking past each other.

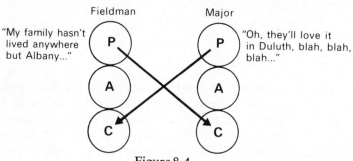

Figure 8.4

In back of John's benign, caring Parent is the Critical Parent who knows he controls all the alternatives, but he also knows better than to bring that out directly. Still, he brings Andrew in there, after arousing high expectations, and now offers what comes across to him as little more than a distasteful relocation. His Critical Parent has Andrew's Child cornered. At one level he is saying, "We're offering you a promotion." On the other, he's saying, "You've got to take it." His game of *Corner* goes like this:

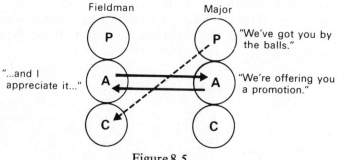

Figure 8.5

There is no move that Andrew can make, other than to comply. There is very little time. Even his desperate attempt to buy a little more time with a stall is met by the foregone conclusion.

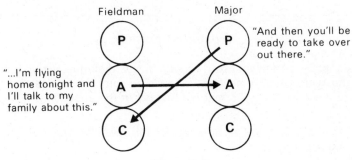

Figure 8.6

It is extremely unlikely that John is aware of his Critical Parent. It operates without his Adult checking into its source or the effect it produces on others. Indeed, the only evidence he has for it is in poor Andy's perception. To such a bland Parent, which is operating for the good of his employee as well as the company, such a response could only be regarded as a sign of immaturity. After all, "We didn't make this decision suddenly..."

However, Andy's perception is itself a reality which must be dealt with if communication and problem solving are to take place. If John's Adult were reading Andy's responses—"It's sort of tough...," "And there's my house...," "Just what *is* my position...?"—these could be checked out and the two men could be brought into a genuine exchange. As it is, there are parts of the dialogue which simply do not fit together.

The pieces which don't fit are John's assumption that he controls all the alternatives and Andrew's assumption that he should be involved in the decision making process. The very least he might hold out for is that his feelings should be considered, but he really wants more than that.

John has kept his eye on the ponderous bureaucratic process, but for his employee's Parent, Adult and Child he has a blind spot. The consequent breakdown in communications, which starts with a few broken threads, ends with a huge rip torn through their relationship. The power exercised by John is not in itself negative, but when it is applied to increasing resistance, the negative results multiply.

Knowing these things, what would you do now to increase the probability of having your employee accept relocation without loss of morale?

## Awareness Format

Revise the script by writing your own version of this dialogue, which has ended so badly. Use the Awareness Format to do it, and then compare your version with ours. A sample for the Awareness Format is provided in the appendix.

### I. Tapes
Change John's Child tape ("I'll do whatever you say." "My feelings don't count.") into an Adult statement.

Adult: _____

_____

Change John's Parent tape ("Take care of your boys.") into an Adult statement.

Adult: _____

_____

### II. Key Crossed Transaction
Change the crossed transaction (see Fig. 8.1) to make it complementary.

John:_____

_____

Andy: _____

_____

### III. Ulterior Message
Change John's Ulterior Message ("We've got you by the balls.") into an Adult statement.

Adult: _____

_____

### IV. Role
Change what John said in his Persecutor/Rescuer role to an Adult statement. Persecutor/Rescuer: "Oh, they'll love it in Duluth, great schools, good people out there..."

Adult: _____

_____

_____

_____

## V. Style

On a scale from 1 to 10 grade the applicability of each criterion from John's point of view. (See the introduction to this book for a detailed explanation of the criteria.)

Grade
1 to 10

A. A Developmental style may be effective:

1. The Adult is available in the other person. _____

2. A joint decision is important. _____

3. An impasse has been reached and a new approach is desired. _____

4. There is time for study and discussion. _____

B. A Controlling style may be effective:

1. The chief priority is to get the task done as soon as possible. _____

2. You intend to direct the project in your own way. _____

3. Ready assent is forthcoming from the other person's Child. _____

4. Negotiation is futile, and you control all the alternatives. _____

C. A Relinquishing style may be effective:

1. The other person has relevant information which you do not possess. _____

2. The other person's Child is upset and needs your Nurturing Parent. _____

3. Development of the other person's autonomy is the most important objective. _____

4. The other person is autonomous, yet a caring relationship still exists. _____

D. A Defensive style may be effective:

1. Your Child is confused or frustrated. _____

2. Participation is against the moral standards of your Parent. _____

3. Your support is not required. _____

4. You are aware that games are being played. _____

Fill in the criteria score chart below according to the numbers indicated for each style. Use the criteria score chart to select a transactional style which is designed to effectively achieve John's Desired Result.

Criteria Score Chart

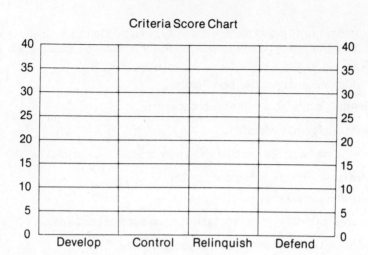

If another style is graded close to the highest one on your chart, you may want to incorporate that in your approach. Both may be appropriate at different times in the dialogue or discussion.

*Strategy*

1. What style is indicated for the Improved Dialogue? _____

_____

2. Make some notes on how John's strategy might be improved, using the style indicated.

_____

_____

_____

_____

_____

_____

_____

_____

_____

_____

Now read the Improved Dialogue and compare it with what you have written in Sections I through V.

## THE IMPROVED DIALOGUE
### Employee Relocation with Minor Promotion

John Major's problem in this transaction is a difficult one to solve, since the groundwork for the conversation has not been done, and what little background *has* been developed has been disastrous. Harry, the division manager concerned, is mentioned only briefly in the dialogue, but his damaging work is evident throughout.

Since there has to be a place where the buck stops, John Major must accept responsibility for having put Harry on the wrong track. It becomes self-evident that while there is a management policy to make this type of decision at high levels, Harry was not asked to sound out Andrew's feelings about being transplanted, nor was he told how to handle informing Andrew of the upcoming interview. Possibly part of the solution to the problem John finds facing him now would be solved in the future by better management techniques on John's part. For example, he could develop more of a propensity to delegate a bit of the authority he clings to almost fanatically.

Now, John Major is faced with the situation as it exists, and the dialogue could easily go the way we originally presented it. It appears very clear after our analysis that is is necessary for John to communicate with Andrew's Adult—and to contact that Adult, he will need to take risks and make blunt approaches that, at least to some extent, ease the errors already made. He could try it this way:

**Major:** How was the flight from Albany, Andy?

**Fieldman:** Kinda bumpy. I never liked flying anyway... It's a lucky thing, I guess, that my territory can be handled by a guy with a car... (*Laughs*)

**Major:** (*Joins in laughter*) Yeah, I suppose so, Andy. Listen, the first thing I want to tell you is that we're talking here today because of the great job you're doing.

**Fieldman:** Thanks.

**Major:** I know your division manager told you I wanted to see you about a promotion. Straight out, it's a promotion to Account Manager with a $4,000 increase, more responsibility, more fringe benefits... but one problem area that I think you can handle.

**Fieldman:** Hey, that sounds good... To tell the truth, though, the way Harry was talking I had the feeling that he was setting me up to take his job...

**Major:** Some day, I have no doubt you will be a division manager. This promotion is a step in that direction. It's a spot where the company needs your abilities.

**Fieldman:** OK, John... That's a great buildup and it is good to hear... but there has to be a catch.

**Major:** (*Light laugh*) Not a catch, Andy. The job requires relocation to Duluth. That's the problem I talked about and the company is ready to do what it has to do to make it as easy as possible for you.

**Fieldman:** Duluth? Hey... wow... How soon am I supposed to make the decision?

**Major:** I was hoping you'd be ready to take over out there a week from today... Now, before you tell me that's unreasonable or too quick, let me say that we don't expect you to move your family out there lock stock and barrel this week... (*Laugh*)

**Fieldman:** (*Weak laugh*) I should hope not.

**Major:** You can handle the territory as if it were an out-of-town series of trips for a month or so while you find the right spot for a home, and while you dispose of your place in Albany. The fact is, Andy, that territory hasn't been handled right and it's a compliment to you that top management feels you're the one guy we all feel can turn it around.

**Fieldman:** Gee, John, you make it hard to bring up my personal problems... I mean, putting it that way... but I could face some family problems on this. My daughter is going to graduate from high school next year... and...

**Major:** Andy, this is an important career step for you. You know better than I do how to handle the matter with your family but I can say this—the financial reward should help make the readjustment a lot easier than it might otherwise be. This isn't your last step up... but it is a very important one.

**Fieldman:** What about my New York territory?

**Major:** We knew that you'd worry about it. And we certainly didn't want you to have both territories on your back, so we've made arrangements for your New York territory to be handled by a new man that Harry will work with directly.

**Fieldman:** You sure had this all planned... Why wasn't I brought into any of the discussion before this?

**Major:** How could we do that? Offer you a "maybe" promotion? Andy, you're management oriented. You understand that decisions like this can't become the subject of the rumor mill... They have to bo solid and ready to act on before they become conversation pieces!

**Fieldman:** Yeah, that's fair enough. Look, let me call my wife now and sort of warm things up for the big pow-wow at home tomorrow... and can we take some time tonight to check over the problem accounts in Duluth?

## Awareness Format Applied to Your Own Situation

**I. Background**
Describe briefly a situation in which you have had a responsible part and are not satisfied with the results:

_____

_____

_____

**II. Desired Result**
What was your Desired Result? _____

_____

**III. Key Crossed Transaction**
In that situation identify a key crossed transaction in which the response came from the Parent or the Child in the other person.

What you said: _____

_____

The response: _____

_____

Diagram your crossed transaction:

**IV. Tapes**
Imagine yourself as you were when you were a very young child and think of an experience which is similar to the one you have just described. Be aware of the people who appear in your mind's eye, what you felt and what you were trying to say to them.

In the recent situation which you have just described, what appears to be the Child tape influencing your behavior from that old scene in your past?

Child tape: _____

_____

Change your Child tape into an Adult statement:

Adult: _____

_____

What appears to be your Parent tape? If you need to, go back to the memory you just retrieved for an awareness of that tape.

Parent tape: _____

_____

Change your Parent tape into an Adult statement:

Adult: _____

_____

## V. Ulterior Message

What Ulterior Message did you send to the other person? You can spot your Ulterior Message by examining your Parent and Child tapes to see how they exerted a negative influence on your transactional style in that situation.

Your Ulterior Message: _____

_____

## VI. Basic Life Position

Check out your feelings in that situation. What Basic Life Position do they seem to indicate?

Check one:  □ I'm not-OK—you're OK.
            □ I'm not-OK—you're not-OK.
            □ I'm OK—you're not-OK.
            □ I'm OK—you're OK.

What is the feeling? _____

## VII. Game Awareness

Now you can see how the parts of your game fall into place. Write here your Desired Result (see II above).

_____

Write here your Ulterior Message (see V above).

_____

Write here the response you got in the crossed transaction (see III above).

_____

Write here your Basic Life Position in that situation (see VI above) and the feeling that goes with it.

Basic Life Position:_____

Feeling: _____

What game seems to be indicated here?

Name: _____

To get out of that game, change your Ulterior Message in that game into an Adult statement.

Adult: _____

_____

## VIII. Role

What role were you playing in that game? Check one:

☐ Persecutor    ☐ Victim    ☐ Rescuer

Describe what you said or did to play that role.

_____

_____

Change that to an Adult behavior or statement:

Adult: _____

_____

## IX. Style

On a scale from 1 to 10 grade the applicability of each criterion from your point of view. (See the introduction to this book for a detailed explanation of the criteria.)

Grade
1 to 10

A. A Developmental style may be effective:

    1. The Adult is available in the other person.      _____

    2. A joint decision is important.      _____

    3. An impasse has been reached and a new approach is desired.      _____

    4. There is time for study and discussion.      _____

B. A Controlling style may be effective:

   1. The chief priority is to get the task done as soon as possible.    _____

   2. You intend to direct the project in your own way.    _____

   3. Ready assent is forthcoming from the other person's Child.    _____

   4. Negotiation is futile, and you control all the alternatives.    _____

C. A Relinquishing style may be effective:

   1. The other person has relevant information which you do not possess.    _____

   2. The other person's Child is upset and needs your Nurturing Parent.    _____

   3. Development of the other person's autonomy is the most important objective.    _____

   4. The other person is autonomous, yet a caring relationship still exists.    _____

D. A Defensive style may be effective:

   1. Your Child is confused or frustrated.    _____

   2. Participation is against the moral standards of your Parent.    _____

   3. Your support is not required.    _____

   4. You are aware that games are being played.    _____

Fill in the criteria score chart below, Use the criteria score chart to develop a transactional strategy that will effectively attain your Desired Result.

Criteria Score Chart

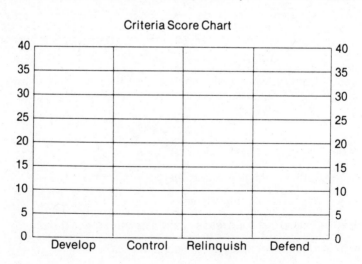

If some other style appears to be close to another one on your chart, you may want to incorporate that in your approach. Both may be appropriate at different times in the dialogue or discussion.

### Strategy

1. What style is indicated for your Improved Dialogue?

_____

2. Look over carefully what you have written in Sections I-IX and use it to help yourself decide how to implement that style. Then make some notes on what you will do:

_____

_____

_____

_____

_____

_____

_____

_____

_____

_____

_____

3. When will you do it? _____

_____

# CHAPTER NINE

# I got nothin' against them jigs...

**Subject:** Seeking more subordinate help
**Initiator:** Employee
**Point of View:** Employee
**Desired Result:** To have additional help granted without downgrading
          of personal efficiency
**Employee:** Harry McPush    **Employer:** Lorna Brubacher

Harry McPush is traffic manager for the Purple Prose Publishing Co. His job consists of seeing that the books they publish are shipped to retail outlets. Lorna Brubacher is Operations Manager. Lorna comes to the shipping department and speaks to Harry across his desk.

**Lorna:** Listen, I came to check on the Pornopalace order from Beverly Hills...

**Harry:** Yeah, I saw it around here, I'll get to it when I can...

**Lorna:** Well, it's important.

**Harry:** Terrific. Everything around here is important. Listen, Lorna, I wanna tell you something straight out. I do one hell of a job, right?

**Lorna:** So?

**Harry:** I mean, you won't say that I don't work my head off getting the stuff out of here...

**Lorna:** You do fine, Harry. About that Pornopalace order...

**Harry:** Well, never mind that for now... I gotta talk to you about something serious.

**Lorna:** Harry, that goddam Pornopalace order is about 20 grand. That's pretty damn serious. Now what about it?

**Harry:** OK, OK, shit, I got the thing out yesterday, OK? Satisfied? Ha, I thought that would grab you! It's amazing how I get the stuff out of here without any help!

**Lorna:** You could have told me that in the first place. See ya... (*Turns to leave*)

**Harry:** (*Grabs her sleeve*) Wait a goddam minute! I told you I had something important to talk about... Whatsamatter, ain't I important enough to waste any time with me or somethin'?

**Lorna:** OK, don't tear the material. What's your beef?

**Harry:** I gotta have an assistant.

**Lorna:** You've been handling this job yourself for about three years, Harry.

**Harry:** Yeah. We had 58 accounts when I took it over, we got 132 now!

**Lorna:** And you've got the automatic tyer and bundling machine now, and the preaddressed labels from accounting...

**Harry:** Big fuckin deal!

**Lorna:** Watch your mouth, mister...

**Harry:** Oh, shit, I could always talk straight to you, Lorna... Now what the hell... You trying to tell me you think I wanna goof off or something?

**Lorna:** I'm telling you this isn't the time or place for...

**Harry:** Whatdya want me to do—make an appointment? Boy, you are really pulling rank around here lately! I know what you think. You think that I'm getting lazy or slow or some goddam thing and that's why I want another body around here, that's what you think.

**Lorna:** No, Harry, I just...

**Harry:** What about Foster in the bindery, huh? He just got an assistant, right? What is that? Because he's black, right, they get all the goodies, right, I bet he got a raise too...

**Lorna:** I think this had gone far enough.

**Harry:** OK, I'll even take a nigger assistant, just to show I ain't got anything against 'em. I mean, you know me, Lorna.

**Lorna:** I'm not so damn sure I did up to now.

**Harry:** OK, never mind he's a jig, is it fair that Foster gets more help and I sweat my things offa me by myself? I been doing good work around here and I ain't got nobody that can say I rub 'em the wrong way.

**Lorna:** Possibly, I now realize, *because* you work alone...

**Harry:** What the hell does that mean? Oh, you're kidding, right? (*Laugh*) Look, Lorna, I didn't mean to sort of hold you here but I just want a fair shake...

**Lorna:** Come to my office first chance you get this afternoon, Harry. I definitely want to get this straightened out.

**Harry:** Hey, OK, Lorna. And forget what I said about those jigs and all... (*Laugh*) I ain't even bigoted about women executives... (*Laugh*) See ya...

## ANALYSIS: NOBODY CARES ABOUT ME
### Seeking More Subordinate Help

**Script Theme:** "Nobody cares about me."

**Tapes:** Parent—"Don't trust 'em." "Try to keep up."
Child—"I feel left out."

**Key Crossed Transaction:** See Fig. 9.1

**Ulterior Message:** "You don't love me."

**Basic Life Position:** "I'm not-OK—you're not-OK."

**Games:** *Harried, Mine Is Bigger than Yours*

**Role:** Victim ("It's amazing how I get stuff out of here without help.")

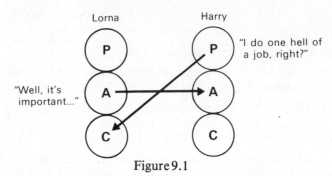

Figure 9.1

Harry McPush was not appreciated, not even *accepted* by his mother. His Child ego state still believes that all women reject him. Actually his mother was just a busy, tired person who held a part-time job at a millinery store, in the shipping department, to keep things going because his father drank too much. She loved him—or at least did not deliberately reject him—but simply did not have the energy to show him much affection due to the heavy problems she had to cope with. Harry was the youngest of five boys. His Child of long ago never forgets that a woman in authority lets you down.

Lorna Brubacher is not an evil woman. She is an efficient, well-organized, intelligent manager. But Harry's Adult is not available to see that. When he looks at Lorna he sees tired, old, grumbly ma who wants no more lovin'! Harry's Child had hoped that working in a porno publishing company would offer some goodies with its sex queens in mini-skirts and even more (or less). But as it often is with hope, this was just a way of manufacturing despair.

Perhaps Lorna's Parent tapes fit in all too well with Harry's Child. She's too concerned with business to have time for him. But there is no deliberate attempt on her part to put him down. She is not even aware of the effect of her behavior on him.

But all that is really his problem, not hers. He is the one who is responsible for that effect and for what he does with it. However, *he* is not aware of *that* either. He really believes that "nobody cares about me" as if indeed it were reality itself. He actually uses bits and pieces of reality to support this view, as in the following transaction:

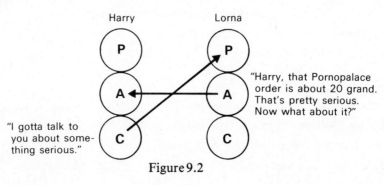

Figure 9.2

He discounts Lorna's intelligence and sound business aggressiveness and sees her from his Child as only aggressively hostile toward him.

The action tilts toward disaster when Harry's Parent comes out to defend his Child from what he perceives as an attack. Actually Lorna is coming from her Adult asking for information. However, Harry does not give her the information which it is later disclosed he has.

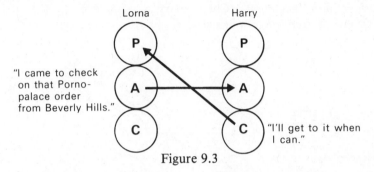

Figure 9.3

Unfortunately for the results, her Parent responds to his, not with an attack, but with a controlling statement in the attempt to persuade Harry about the seriousness of the matter. He resists and it comes out in a defensive move from his Parent to protect his Child.

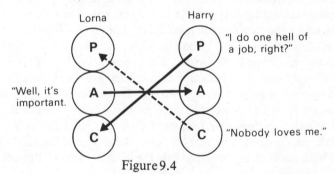

Figure 9.4

Her attempt to get the information she needs is stifled at the moment because his Adult is not available. All his energy is caught up in his Parent protecting his Child. But the protection, like the one he grew up with, is phoney. It's really a rip-off. Like protection in the underworld, it requires a payoff. The payoff is the brown stamps he collects in hurt feelings at being rejected. That is why he's working alone. His punitive Parent drives people away and the little kid inside him is at a loss as to why they go away. He keeps looking for the princess and keeps finding the wicked queen, who gives him the candied apple full of poison. In the real world he gets it from the half-pint flask just barely seen bulging in his hip pocket.

Basically, he is trying to get across his not-OK feelings about being alone and his perception that he is somehow the victim. If it suits that purpose, he will say the order has not gone out yet (because he doesn't have enough help), or if it suits the same purpose better he will say that he got it out yesterday and "it's amazing how I get the stuff out of here without any help!"

Actually, he's not concerned with information at all, but with feelings, and how those feelings can con people into behaving in certain ways. If he plays the game of *Harried* with sufficient proficiency, he will justify his belief that he is "overworked" (Parent tape) and "neglected" (Child tape).

His game of *Harried* goes like this:

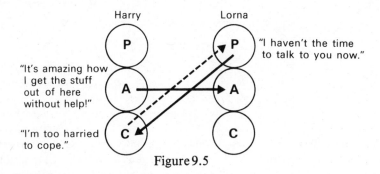

Figure 9.5

Lorna responds to his "not-OK" Child as an unavailable Parent. Her withdrawal is not intentionally a put-down. Rather, it is simply a practical way of dealing with a meeting which she does not feel it is appropriate for her to attend at that time. Harry, however, collects his payoff of bad feelings out of her neglect for his apparent need.

His game of *Mine Is Bigger than Yours* consists of how his *problem* is bigger than Foster's or anyone else's. His game does not achieve the Desired Result, which is to get additional help. It only ends, like *Harried*, in bad feelings. He is seeking to solve his problem from his Child, which is not a problem solver. He is not aware that feelings do not change anything. He tries hard, but that is as far as it goes. The negative feelings he gets are so strong that his Adult is decommissioned. All the energy is there in his Child, reaffirming his Basic Life Position, which is "I'm not-OK—you're not-OK."

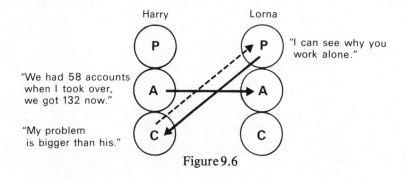

Figure 9.6

Harry's games keep him in his familiar role of Victim, which fits well into the perennial theme of his loser's script, "Nobody cares about me." If he engaged himself in constructive change, he would have to face such things as a responsible attitude toward women in authority and possible intimacy, a responsible attitude toward himself and the possibility of success in his life and work. All that is too scary for his Child, who would rather blame others than take any such risk. The poisoned apple in his pocket is his Parent's protection. Failure and success teach him nothing. They only reaffirm his script in the way the strokes get handed out.

How would you change the dialogue if you were Harry and aware of these things?

## Awareness Format

Revise the script by writing your own version of this dialogue, which has ended so badly. Use the Awareness Format to do it, and then compare your version with ours. A sample for the Awareness Format is provided in the appendix.

### I. Tapes
Change Harry's Child tape ("I feel left out.") into an Adult statement.

Adult: _____

_____

Change Harry's Parent tape ("Don't trust 'em." "Try to keep up.") into an Adult statement.

Adult: _____

_____

### II. Key Crossed Transaction
Change the crossed transaction (see Fig. 9.1) to make it complementary.

Harry: _____

_____

Lorna: _____

_____

### III. Ulterior Message
Change Harry's Ulterior Message ("You don't love me.") into an Adult statement.

Adult: _____

_____

### IV. Role
Change what Harry said in his Victim role to an Adult statement.
Victim: "It's amazing how I get stuff out of here without help."

Adult: _____

_____

## V. Style

On a scale from 1 to 10 grade the applicability of each criterion from Harry's point of view. (See the introduction to this book for a detailed explanation of the criteria.)

Grade
1 to 10

A. A Developmental style may be effective:

   1. The Adult is available in the other person. _____

   2. A joint decision is important. _____

   3. An impasse has been reached and a new approach is desired. _____

   4. There is time for study and discussion. _____

B. A Controlling style may be effective:

   1. The chief priority is to get the task done as soon as possible. _____

   2. You intend to direct the project in your own way. _____

   3. Ready assent is forthcoming from the other person's Child. _____

   4. Negotiation is futile, and you control all the alternatives. _____

C. A Relinquishing style may be effective:

   1. The other person has relevant information which you do not possess. _____

   2. The other person's Child is upset and needs your Nurturing Parent. _____

   3. Development of the other person's autonomy is the most important objective. _____

   4. The other person is autonomous, yet a caring relationship still exists. _____

D. A Defensive style may be effective:

   1. Your Child is confused or frustrated. _____

   2. Participation is against the moral standards of your Parent. _____

   3. Your support is not required. _____

   4. You are aware that games are being played. _____

Fill in the criteria score chart below according to the numbers indicated for each style. Use the criteria score chart to select a transactional style which is designed to effectively achieve Harry's Desired Result.

Criteria Score Chart

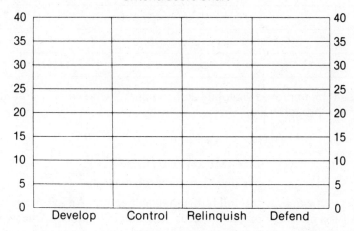

|   | Develop | Control | Relinquish | Defend |
|---|---------|---------|------------|--------|

If another style is graded close to the highest one on your chart, you may want to incorporate that in your approach. Both may be appropriate at different times in the dialogue or discussion.

*Strategy*

1. What style is indicated for the Improved Dialogue? _____

_____

2. Make some notes on how Harry's strategy might be improved, using the style indicated.

_____

_____

_____

_____

_____

_____

_____

_____

_____

---

---

---

---

Now read the Improved Dialogue and compare it with what you have written in Sections I through V.

## THE IMPROVED DIALOGUE
### Seeking More Subordinate Help

An optimist sees a glass as half full rather than half empty. An idiotic optimist sees an earthquake as a blessing because it speeds urban redevelopment. One would have to be classified as the latter to seek a turnaround of drastic proportions in the character of Harry McPush. We have to seek here a great deal of strength and perception on the part of Lorna Brubacher to salvage this very difficult fellow.

It is obvious that McPush would in no way submit to TA training without strong incentive. By no means would he initiate it or even have heard of it. TA isn't an essential part of the plots of the latest in pornographic novels.

Dear, innocent reader, if you see any part of yourself in this McPush individual... deep self-examination is called for... stet! It would be difficult to accept the premise that any of those reading this treatise are as far gone as McPush... therefore, as your Adult recognizes the McPush elements in your attitude, you have a marvelous opportunity that... we hope... Lorna Brubacher will provide (as far as possible) to Harry McPush.

The logical outcome of the encounter analyzed would be the replacement of Harry McPush. But Lorna Brubacher is a bright, well-organized executive. She recognizes that McPush, in his own way, indeed *does* do a very good job. She will therefore take steps to have him take TA training at company expense before she exposes an assistant to his tender care.

For the purposes of our exercise, let us then assume that Lorna had noticed McPush's difficulties in relating prior to this conversation and provided him with TA insights. It would be a ridiculous assumption to think that he would have made a spontaneous effort in that direction. Even after TA training, we cannot expect a miraculous metamorphosis... but, remember, Lorna is aware of his attitude.

**Lorna:** Listen, I came to check on that Pornopalace order from Beverly Hills...

**Harry:** Yeah, I saw it around here... Wait a minute, lemme check...

**Lorna:** It's important.

**Harry:** Yeah, everything around here is important. Hey... here it is... I got the Pornopalace order out yesterday. Hey, Lorna, I do a heck of a job around here, right?

**Lorna:** I've got no complaints, Harry.

**Harry:** I mean, you won't say that I don't work my head off getting the stuff out of here...

**Lorna:** Never said that, and you know it. You do a fine job.

**Harry:** OK, but I gotta break my bippy to do it... and to get that Pornopalace order out, I wanna tell you I had to move back a couple of smaller orders.

**Lorna:** That's OK, Pornopalace was the only rush deal in the house.

**Harry:** Look, Lorna, let me say it straight out. I need an assistant.

**Lorna:** I wasn't aware the load was getting that heavy... You've been handling this job yourself for about three years.

**Harry:** Yeah. We had 58 accounts when I took over and we got 132 now!

**Lorna:** I was under the impression that the preaddressed labels from accounting and the new tying machine helped take off some of the pressure.

**Harry:** Well, it hasn't been enough. You don't think I'd ask for an assistant just because I want to goof off, do you?

**Lorna:** Of course not... but I don't think right now is the time to talk about it.

**Harry:** Whatdya want me to do, make an appointment?... Boy, you are really pulling rank around here lately.

**Lorna:** Hold it, Harry. Do you really believe that?

**Harry:** Well, naw, I guess I'm just uptight about that assistant thing... I mean Foster in the bindery just got an assistant and I gotta wonder... is it 'cause he's black? I mean those people get special treatment lately...

**Lorna:** Foster has an assistant because he asked for one—we got together, talked it out, and figured out that his department could operate more efficiently if an assistant were hired. It's that simple.

**Harry:** Great. OK,... I'll buy that... So what about me?

**Lorna:** Same ball of wax, Harry. If you can make it, come to my office about three this afternoon, and bring your traffic records. We can sit down and analyze the situation together... and if it warrants another employee, that can be done.

**Harry:** That sounds reasonable... My bein' white won't count against me will it? (*Nervous laugh*)

**Lorna:** No, but it won't count for you either. All we want is the facts, right, Harry?

**Harry:** Yes, ma'am, just the facts, ma'am. (*Laughs*) See you at three.

## Awareness Format Applied to Your Own Situation

### I. Background
Describe briefly a situation in which you have had a responsible part and are not satisfied with the results:

_____

_____

_____

### II. Desired Result
What was your Desired Result? _____

_____

### III. Key Crossed Transaction
In that situation identify a key crossed transaction in which the response came from the Parent or the Child in the other person.

What you said: _____

_____

The response: _____

_____

Diagram your crossed transaction:

### IV. Tapes
Imagine yourself as you were when you were a very young child and think of an experience which is similar to the one you have just described. Be aware of the people who appear in your mind's eye, what you felt and what you were trying to say to them.

In the recent situation which you have just described, what appears to be the Child tape influencing your behavior from that old scene in your past?

Child tape:  _____

_____

Change your Child tape into an Adult statement:

Adult:  _____

_____

What appears to be your Parent tape? If you need to, go back to the memory you just retrieved for an awareness of that tape.

Parent tape:  _____

_____

Change your Parent tape into an Adult statement:

Adult:  _____

_____

## V. Ulterior Message

What Ulterior Message did you send to the other person? You can spot your Ulterior Message by examining your Parent and Child tapes to see how they exerted a negative influence on your transactional style in that situation.

Your Ulterior Message:  _____

_____

## VI. Basic Life Position

Check out your feelings in that situation. What Basic Life Position do they seem to indicate?

Check one:  ☐ I'm not-OK—you're OK.
☐ I'm not-OK—you're not-OK.
☐ I'm OK—you're not-OK.
☐ I'm OK—you're OK.

What is the feeling?  _____

## VII. Game Awareness

Now you can see how the parts of your game fall into place. Write here your Desired Result (see II above).

_____

Write here your Ulterior Message (see V above).

_____

Write here the response you got in the crossed transaction (see III above).

_____

Write here your Basic Life Position in that situation (see VI above) and the feeling that goes with it.

Basic Life Position: _____

Feeling: _____

What game seems to be indicated here?

Name: _____

To get out of that game, change your Ulterior Message in that game into an Adult statement.

Adult: _____

_____

## VIII. Role
What role were you playing in that game? Check one:

☐ Persecutor   ☐ Victim   ☐ Rescuer

Describe what you said or did to play that role.

_____

_____

Change that to an Adult behavior or statement:

Adult: _____

_____

## IX. Style
On a scale from 1 to 10 grade the applicability of each criterion from your point of view. (See the introduction to this book for a detailed explanation of the criteria.)

Grade
1 to 10

A. A Developmental style may be effective:

1. The Adult is available in the other person.          _____

2. A joint decision is important.                        _____

3. An impasse has been reached and a new approach is desired.    _____

4. There is time for study and discussion.               _____

B. A Controlling style may be effective:

1. The chief priority is to get the task done as soon as possible. _____

2. You intend to direct the project in your own way. _____

3. Ready assent is forthcoming from the other person's Child. _____

4. Negotiation is futile, and you control all the alternatives. _____

C. A Relinquishing style may be effective:

1. The other person has relevant information which you do not possess. _____

2. The other person's Child is upset and needs your Nurturing Parent. _____

3. Development of the other person's autonomy is the most important objective. _____

4. The other person is autonomous, yet a caring relationship still exists. _____

D. A Defensive style may be effective:

1. Your Child is confused or frustrated. _____

2. Participation is against the moral standards of your Parent. _____

3. Your support is not required. _____

4. You are aware that games are being played. _____

Fill in the criteria score chart below, Use the criteria score chart to develop a transactional strategy that will effectively attain your Desired Result.

Criteria Score Chart

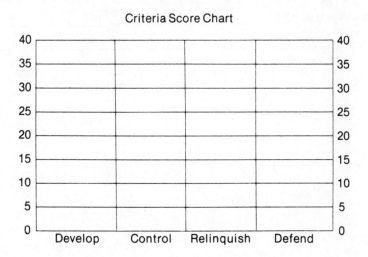

If some other style appears to be close to another one on your chart, you may want to incorporate that in your approach. Both may be appropriate at different times in the dialogue or discussion.

*Strategy*

1. What style is indicated for your Improved Dialogue?

_____

2. Look over carefully what you have written in Sections I-IX and use it to help yourself decide how to implement that style. Then make some notes on what you will do:

_____
_____
_____
_____
_____
_____
_____
_____
_____
_____
_____

3. When will you do it? _____

_____

# SECTION THREE
# Sales

# CHAPTER TEN

# We handle the whole thing...

**Subject:** Selling an intangible or service
**Initiator:** Salesman
**Point of View:** Salesman
**Desired Result:** a) Making the sale
　　　　　　　　b) (Less desirable) Leaving the relationship strong
　　　　　　　　　　for another interview
**Salesman:** Dave Closer　　　**Customer:** Irving Armadillo

Dave Closer works for the Artsycraft Communications Development Organization. He has a very large portfolio under his arm as he comes into Armadillo's office. Armadillo is Director of Sales Promotion for the Femhigh Company, manufacturer of fast selling Femlube Douches and related products.

**Closer:** My card, Mr. Armadillo. I'm Dave Closer.

**Armadillo:** Nice to meet you, Closer. Sit down. What do you have to show me?

**Closer:** (*Sits*) Well, I've got some things I'm sure you'll be interested in seeing. But do you have anything pending right now that I could help you with?

**Armadillo:** I have a lot of things pending, which is why it took so long to give you this appointment. But I would like to know what it is your company does.

**Closer:** We handle your communications, we do sales promotion, we plan campaigns and carry them through all the way.

**Armadillo:** You say you "do sales promotion." What exactly does that mean?

**Closer:** Why, it means we handle the whole thing. You have a sales promotion project, we take it and carry the ball! Like we handled the free kite promotion for the Budgetary State Bank last year...

**Armadillo:** We aren't in the banking business. Be specific. What exactly do you *do*?

**Closer:** Say you have a product that you want to promote. We take that product and write the copy, do the color comps, I mean we finish it all the way.

**Armadillo:** You're offering me a writing and layout service?

**Closer:** Yes, but that's just sort of part of it. I mean I want to emphasize that we are a complete marketing communications organization.

**Armadillo:** Assuming I stipulate that, could you tell me precisely what it is you do physically. Like, when I hand you a rough layout, what happens?

**Closer:** First thing, we have our creative department give it a professional touch.

**Armadillo:** I do those roughs myself and I'm a professional. With that out of the way, what exactly can you do for us?

**Closer:** Everything you need! We handle the art work, right to the finished mechanical.

**Armadillo:** Fine. Do you have your own typesetting equipment in house?

**Closer:** Just as good! Why we're the biggest customer for one of the best typesetters in the city...

**Armadillo:** Let me save you some time. Apparently you don't know a lot about our operation... Briefly, we lay out all our promotional printed material and all we're interested in is production work...

**Closer:** (*Laugh*) You mean you never have any use for outside ideas? You do all the creative work yourself?

**Armadillo:** Yes I do, and no I don't, to answer your questions in order. But I decide where I look for creative work and right now I want to know if there are specific physical jobs your company would like to do for us. Can you just give me that information?

**Closer:** Sure, sure, we're as interested in the unimportant pasteup job as we are in doing a real job of sales promotion.

**Armadillo:** I'm thrilled.

**Closer:** Would you like to look at some of the things we've done?

**Armadillo:** Yes, but let's move along, I have a meeting in seven minutes.

**Closer:** (*Opening portfolio*) Now I have here a promotional project that we handled all the way. Notice the miniature Eiffel Tower that pops up when you open the brochure... in full color with fluorescent touches at the top...

**Armadillo:** That's for an architectural firm...

**Closer:** Oh, I realise it doesn't relate directly to feminine hygiene, but I wanted you to see it to realize that the same kind of creativity...

**Armadillo:** It's time for my meeting. Thank you for coming in. I'll put your card in my file. Goodbye.


### ANALYSIS: HE DOESN'T KNOW HIS CLIENT
#### Selling an Intangible or Service

**Script Theme:** "I'm trying so hard to please you."

**Tapes:** Parent—"Knock 'em dead." "Make a good impression."
         Child —"Spank me."

**Key Crossed Transaction:**

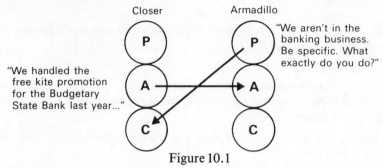

Figure 10.1

**Ulterior Message:** "Tell me I'm stupid."

**Basic Life Position:** "I'm not-OK—you're OK."

**Games:** *Corner, Stupid*

**Role:** Rescuer ("Everything you need.")
      Victim  ("Now I have here a promotional project...")

Dave Closer knows his product but not his client. His Adult does not have the basic information to speak intelligently to the needs of Irving Armadillo, consequently he relies on his old tapes in the session. However, he does not see how extremely gamey Armadillo can be in dealing with the average type of sales approach. As a professional creative person, Armadillo does not want to be "sold" anything and becomes extremely defensive when he senses that someone is trying to control him. His Parent comes out to defend his Child. Unfortunately, Closer does not see that in *his* Adult, and so *his* Child takes over and carries the action in what probably tends to be a familiar way with him. Actually, it is doubtful, in the brief time he's got with Armadillo, that he could really get through to him and make a sale. If he were aware of this he could shift gears and obtain another option.

The stimulus that first hooks Armadillo's wily Parent is the slight but powerful slur in Closer's phrase "We handle your communications..." Perhaps the misuse of the pronoun "your" comes from Closer's Child, who would *like* to handle *your* communications. At any rate the use of the phrase is inappropriate. Closer has tried to move directly from a ritual to intimacy and winds up being caught in Armadillo's games. For a less gamey type of person the slur would have gone unnoticed; but for Armadillo it comes across in neon lights.

Closer has also missed the very obvious fact that Armadillo is under tremendous pressure. Whatever he offers must be very precise and to the point or it will be lost, simply because Armadillo does not have time to develop ideas. He is looking for finished products that exactly fit into explicit needs that will help him quickly to further his projects. Closer's approach really calls for more time than is available. If his Adult were aware of that fact he could adjust his behavior, but his ponderous Parent goes on with the prescribed program, and his Child gets into games.

Early in the session Closer could have discerned that Armadillo's Adult is going to be hard to reach. Though Closer comes from his Adult, he does not get an Adult response, because he does not have sufficient energy at that level. The real energy, as will later appear, is in his Child.

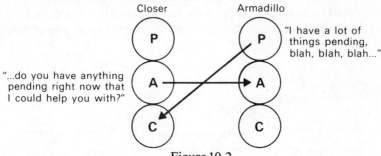

Figure 10.2

Since Closer is dealing with Armadillo's Parent, he is not dealing with one who is truly seeking information, but rather with one who is using questions in a punitive and attacking way. He keeps addressing Armadillo's Adult, but it is simply not available, so the transactions cross, one after another.

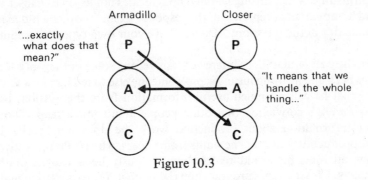

Figure 10.3

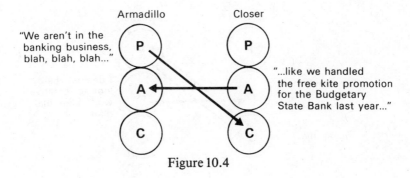

Figure 10.4

Little does Closer see the trap he is falling into. Behind all Armadillo's questions is a game of *NIGYSOB*. His Parent wants to expose, embarrass, and hurt Closer and is waiting until he gets enough of the "right" information to do it. He finds his mark when he gets Closer to talk about doing the layout work—an area in which he himself is expert. Just about any remark Closer makes will play into the hands of Armadillo's Critical Parent. His request for "exactly what can you do for us" is met with a bland "everything you need," and sure enough, Closer is on the Victim side of that game. He is cornered.

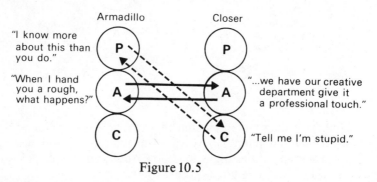

Figure 10.5

But Armadillo is just getting warmed up. He does not let on to Closer what he is up to, and his apparent acceptance in the response "Fine" covers a hidden rejection which comes out in the question: "Do you have your own typesetting equipment in house?"

Apparently all Armadillo is interested in is getting some of the work load off his company's back and he by no means wants someone else to tell him how to do that. It is unlikely that he will get much useful information from this session, but he will justify his *Parent's* conviction that other people aren't much help. Though he is asking for information about production work, he does not specify that it is *uncreative* production work that he wants from Closer, who is selling creative work. If Closer saw all that, he would realize how seriously he is caught in the game. Unfortunately, Closer's tapes program him right into it. He tries hard to make a good impression on Armadillo's Critical Parent, not realizing what he is dealing with.

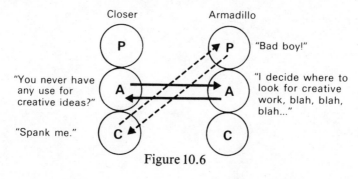

Figure 10.6

The "spank" comes in Armadillo's response "I'm thrilled," which is full of sarcasm. Instead of hearing it in his Adult, however, Closer moves right along into his sales pitch. Unfortunately for him, his Child is programmed to do the very thing which is least useful to him, i.e., to respond directly to the negative remarks from Armadillo's Critical Parent and to come back and ask for more.

Following the Parent tape, to "make a good impression," he plays his trump card with the Eiffel Tower promotional gadget, which then gets zapped. He walks right into it. Armadillo has already made it clear that he is not buying his offer for creative work. Armadillo is in control. Yet Closer tries to take charge of the meeting and to give his creative spiel. To his Child it must seem all too familiar—just like home. To Armadillo's Parent he is just another ant.

If you were Closer, aware of what you were dealing with in that situation, what would you do?

---

### Awareness Format

Revise the script by writing your own version of this dialogue, which has ended so badly. Use the Awareness Format to do it, and then compare your version with ours. A sample for the Awareness Format is provided in the appendix.

#### I. Tapes
Change Closer's Child tape ("Spank me.") into an Adult statement.

Adult: _____

_____

Change Closer's Parent tape ("Knock 'em dead." "Make a good impression.") into an Adult statement.

Adult: _____

_____

#### II. Key Crossed Transaction
Change the crossed transaction (see Fig. 10.1) to make it complementary.

Closer: _____

_____

_____

Armadillo: _____

_____

_____

### III. Ulterior Message

Change Closer's Ulterior Message ("Tell me I'm stupid.") into an Adult statement.

Adult: _____

_____

### IV. Role

Change what Closer said in his Rescuer/Victim role to an Adult statement.

Rescuer: "Everything you need."

Victim: "Now I have here a promotional project..."

Adult: _____

_____

### V. Style

On a scale from 1 to 10 grade the applicability of each criterion from Closer's point of view. (See the introduction to this book for a detailed explanation of the criteria.)

A. A Developmental style may be effective:

Grade 1 to 10

1. The Adult is available in the other person. _____

2. A joint decision is important. _____

3. An impasse has been reached and a new approach is desired. _____

4. There is time for study and discussion. _____

B. A Controlling style may be effective:

1. The chief priority is to get the task done as soon as possible. _____

2. You intend to direct the project in your own way. _____

3. Ready assent is forthcoming from the other person's Child. _____

4. Negotiation is futile, and you control all the alternatives. _____

C. A Relinquishing style may be effective:

1. The other person has relevant information which you do not possess. _____

2. The other person's Child is upset and needs your Nurturing Parent. _____

3. Development of the other person's autonomy is the most important objective. _____

4. The other person is autonomous, yet a caring relationship still exists. _____

D. A Defensive style may be effective:

    1. Your Child is confused or frustrated.      _____

    2. Participation is against the moral standards of your Parent.      _____

    3. Your support is not required.      _____

    4. You are aware that games are being played.      _____

Fill in the criteria score chart below according to the numbers indicated for each style. Use the criteria score chart to select a transactional style which is designed to effectively achieve Closer's Desired Result.

Criteria Score Chart

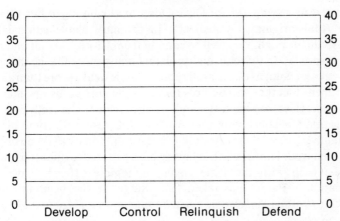

If another style is graded close to the highest one on your chart, you may want to incorporate that in your approach. Both may be appropriate at different times in the dialogue or discussion.

*Strategy*

1. What style is indicated for the Improved Dialogue?   _____

_____

2. Make some notes on how Closer's strategy might be improved, using the style indicated.

_____

_____

---

---

---

Now read the Improved Dialogue and compare it with what you have written in Sections I through V.

## THE IMPROVED DIALOGUE
### Selling an Intangible or Service

It is crystal clear from our analysis that Armadillo's Parent is the sole participant in this dialogue. Neither his Adult nor his Child is really ever invited to take part. As a rather general consideration, the Closers of the world need to be prepared for just this kind of Armadillo.

Our analyst reveals a sympathy for Dave Closer in attributing to him effort after effort to make Adult-originated statements. In ordinary conversational circumstances, those statements might very well be coming from Closer's Adult and result in an Adult-based response. In this case and probably many more like it, the speaking Adult lacks information and, as our analysis points out, is weak. More than all of this, however, is the salient fact that Armadillo's Parent is the part of his personality that meets *any* creative services salesman. It stands as an armed-to-the-teeth protector of Armadillo's time and a barrier to both his Adult and his Child. Early in his career, Armadillo might have greeted these salesfolk with an Adult ready to do business, or a Child ready to be amazed. However, after having been exposed to one after another of these salespeople, each with the same vague, intangible offer to "do creative miracles," Armadillo's Parent has taken full charge of the beginning of each interview. *Breaking through that Parent's guard could be all it takes to make a sale, if not sure, highly likely.*

To find out if indeed he is faced with a Parent-dominated Armadillo, Closer's opening gambit needs to be gently probing. The nature of what Dave is selling has many facets and he needs to determine which of his services Armadillo truly *needs* (and knows he needs). After establishing that, further along in their relationship, it might be possible for Closer to show Armadillo that there are other services he needs that he *doesn't* know he needs.

Not mentioned in the analysis, but of obvious importance, is the fact that Closer needs to be more conversant with Armadillo's business before he ever arrives in this office. Nowhere in the dialogue does Closer relate to the Femlube business nor, indeed, to the entire product marketing area. He provides Armadillo's Parent with reinforced proof that the Closers who call upon him are ill-prepared children who, for their own good, need to be dominated and humiliated.

Now, let's assume that Dave Closer has in fact taken a few moments to determine what business Armadillo is in and is fully aware of the powerful Parent he must face. . .

**Closer:** My card, Mr. Armadillo. I'm Dave Closer.

**Armadillo:** Nice to meet you, Closer. Sit down. What do you have to show me?

**Closer:** (*Sits*) I've got a portfolio full here, but I won't try to go through the whole thing. There *are* a few items there that fit right into marketing to the trade. Before I whip out my fancy stuff, though, can I ask a question or two?

**Armadillo:** For example?

**Closer:** Do you have an in-house art department?

**Armadillo:** No. That's why I took the time to talk to you.

**Closer:** I understand... I asked because in some firms they do have art departments but still put out a good part of their work when the load gets heavy.

**Armadillo:** True. That's a perceptive conclusion, Closer.

**Closer:** OK, then. Let me lay it out for you. Artsycraft Communications can do as much of your sales promotion package as you want done... or as little. To give me a little better picture of how much of a package to offer you, would you let me see a few of your most typical deal sheets or brochures... or any material that you've recently used?

**Armadillo:** Sure, why not. (*Gets some material from files*) I want to warn you that price is a very important factor in our work. (*Hands the material to Closer*) We look for the best quality we can get... for a price.

**Closer:** I think we can be competitive on this type of work. When you hand this work out, Mr. Armadillo, is it already in rough form or do you require that layout and copywriting be provided?

**Armadillo:** I do the copywriting, and I provide complete hand roughs.

**Closer:** Good enough. Then you want typesetting and board work on these types of projects and we're prepared to offer that to you at a good price.

**Armadillo:** Fine. I might add that there are times when I will ask for help in the design and copy areas and I'd expect to pay for that. Basically, though, I'm looking for clean work and fast turnaround... and price.

**Closer:** I'd like the chance to prove to you that we can provide all of that. And I'd personally be handling this account so that in emergencies I can be reached at home... We're not a nine to five, weekdays only operation. We've got a pretty big operation but we try very hard to provide that small-company personal kind of service. Of course, we depend on services like typesetters and artists that work normal hours... What I'm saying is that if I have to rush out here a couple of times a day to keep things moving, or take a copy change at home so that I can get our artist on it first thing in the morning, I'm ready.

**Armadillo:** Don't oversell, Closer. (*Laugh*) You're starting to hook my Critical Parent and I had been giving him a rest. Call me a week from Tuesday and I'll have some deal sheets you can bid on.

## Awareness Format Applied to Your Own Situation

### I. Background
Describe briefly a situation in which you have had a responsible part and are not satisfied with the results:

_____

_____

_____

### II. Desired Result
What was your Desired Result? _____

_____

### III. Key Crossed Transaction
In that situation identify a key crossed transaction in which the response came from the Parent or the Child in the other person.

What you said: _____

_____

The response: _____

_____

Diagram your crossed transaction:

### IV. Tapes
Imagine yourself as you were when you were a very young child and think of an experience which is similar to the one you have just described. Be aware of the people who appear in your mind's eye, what you felt and what you were trying to say to them.

In the recent situation which you have just described, what appears to be the Child tape influencing your behavior from that old scene in your past?

Child tape: _____

_____

Change your Child tape into an Adult statement:

Adult: _____

_____

What appears to be your Parent tape? If you need to, go back to the memory you just retrieved for an awareness of that tape.

Parent tape: _____

_____

Change your Parent tape into an Adult statement:

Adult: _____

_____

## V. Ulterior Message

What Ulterior Message did you send to the other person? You can spot your Ulterior Message by examining your Parent and Child tapes to see how they exerted a negative influence on your transactional style in that situation.

Your Ulterior Message: _____

_____

## VI. Basic Life Position

Check out your feelings in that situation. What Basic Life Position do they seem to indicate?

Check one: ☐ I'm not-OK—you're OK.
            ☐ I'm not-OK—you're not-OK.
            ☐ I'm OK—you're not-OK.
            ☐ I'm OK—you're OK.

What is the feeling? _____

## VII. Game Awareness

Now you can see how the parts of your game fall into place. Write here your Desired Result (see II above).

_____

Write here your Ulterior Message (see V above).

_____

Write here the response you got in the crossed transaction (see III above).

_____

Write here your Basic Life Position in that situation (see VI above) and the feeling that goes with it.

Basic Life Position: _____

Feeling: _____

What game seems to be indicated here?

Name: _____

To get out of that game, change your Ulterior Message in that game into an Adult statement.

Adult: _____

_____

## VIII. Role

What role were you playing in that game? Check one:

☐ Persecutor   ☐ Victim   ☐ Rescuer

Describe what you said or did to play that role.

_____

_____

Change that to an Adult behavior or statement:

Adult: _____

_____

## IX. Style

On a scale from 1 to 10 grade the applicability of each criterion from your point of view. (See the introduction to this book for a detailed explanation of the criteria.)

Grade
1 to 10

A. A Developmental style may be effective:

1. The Adult is available in the other person.   _____

2. A joint decision is important.   _____

3. An impasse has been reached and a new approach is desired.   _____

4. There is time for study and discussion.   _____

B. A Controlling style may be effective:

1. The chief priority is to get the task done as soon as possible. _____

2. You intend to direct the project in your own way. _____

3. Ready assent is forthcoming from the other person's Child. _____

4. Negotiation is futile, and you control all the alternatives. _____

C. A Relinquishing style may be effective:

1. The other person has relevant information which you do not possess. _____

2. The other person's Child is upset and needs your Nurturing Parent. _____

3. Development of the other person's autonomy is the most important objective. _____

4. The other person is autonomous, yet a caring relationship still exists. _____

D. A Defensive style may be effective:

1. Your Child is confused or frustrated. _____

2. Participation is against the moral standards of your Parent. _____

3. Your support is not required. _____

4. You are aware that games are being played. _____

Fill in the criteria score chart below, Use the criteria score chart to develop a transactional strategy that will effectively attain your Desired Result.

Criteria Score Chart

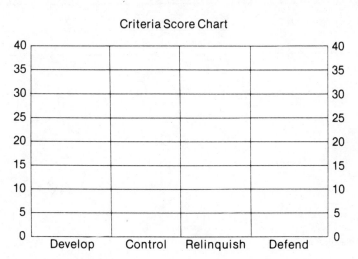

If some other style appears to be close to another one on your chart, you may want to incorporate that in your approach. Both may be appropriate at different times in the dialogue or discussion.

*Strategy*

1. What style is indicated for your Improved Dialogue?

_____

2. Look over carefully what you have written in Sections I-IX and use it to help yourself decide how to implement that style. Then make some notes on what you will do:

_____
_____
_____
_____
_____
_____
_____
_____
_____
_____

3. When will you do it? _____

_____

# CHAPTER ELEVEN

# Guaranteed sale, right?

**Subject:** Selling a product for resale
**Initiator:** Salesman
**Point of View:** Salesman
**Desired Result:** Make the sale and stimulate action to guarantee
highest possible resale
**Salesman:** Prescott Highpower      **Buyer:** Horace Singlemind

Highpower waves to departing salesman as he enters, with Singlemind busy putting away the literature the previous salesman has left. As Highpower gets closer to the desk, Singlemind looks up.

**Highpower:** Horace, how are you? Good to see you again... Looks like you're busy as always, eh? (*Laugh*)

**Singlemind:** (*Perfunctorily grabs Highpower's hand, gestures him to a seat*) Hi.

**Highpower:** You know I've got your regular order in the works, Horace... I want to thank you for giving me this extra time to make a presentation on our new product... and I tell you it is a money-maker!

**Singlemind:** OK, Press, but listen, I really have just five minutes so give it to me straight and fast.

**Highpower:** You know me, Horace, I don't fool around. When I've got something hot, I don't waste a lot of time with preliminaries, I get right to it and when I tell you you ought to have space in your stores for a hot one, man you know I am telling it like it is!

**Singlemind:** The last time you pitched me like this I bought a load of disposable hair curlers. You haven't picked them up yet. Why don't you issue the credit up front?... Let's see... (*Shuffles papers*) I've got 156 dozen to return...

**Highpower:** Hey, look, Horace, everybody has a bomb once in a while, right? We'll take care of those curlers.

**Singlemind:** When?

**Highpower:** Soon as the home office OK's the return... I sent in the request.

**Singlemind:** Six weeks ago. When we get the OK on the return, come in and we'll talk about new stuff.

**Highpower:** Hey, come on, Horace, you know we're OK on that stuff... Takes a little time is all... and I made a special trip to show you the SaniBaby System...

**Singlemind:** OK, OK, show me.

**Highpower:** I've got this flashcard presentation... (*Hunts through his bag as he talks*) Ah, here it is... Just let me set up this stand on your desk... Can we move some of these papers?

**Singlemind:** Is this gonna take a hell of a lot of time? I mean, I wish... Can you cut the preliminaries and get to the meat?

**Highpower:** Yeah, sure... (*Flashing one card after another at terrific speed*) These first twelve cards establish the size of the baby market, but you know that... and here it is, the SaniBaby System!

**Singlemind:** Looks like a sort of diaper holder...

**Highpower:** It's a lot more than that... It's a system for keeping babies dry, with a terrific resale potential and...

**Singlemind:** You mean refills?

**Highpower:** Horace, you sure can get down to cases fast! Right on...

**Singlemind:** That's a hell of a big package... Where will I find shelf space?

**Highpower:** You found shelf space for Pampers, right? Are you sorry? Well, the SaniBaby System is going to hand you more profit than...

**Singlemind:** And I suppose your marketing research people gave you the word that the public is breathlessly waiting for SaniBaby.

**Highpower:** Exactly. The test market results are on the first twelve cards I went through for you... Now as I go on with these cards, you can see that the refills are a much more compact package...

**Singlemind:** All right, Press, skip the rest of those cards... Set up my usual opening order, one dozen systems and refills per A store and we'll see what happens.

**Highpower:** I didn't get to the great floorstand prepack...

**Singlemind:** Not this trip... Guaranteed sale, right?

**Highpower:** Right, and like it says on the sheet, three free with nine...

**Singlemind:** Fine. Process the order as soon as you pick up the hair curlers.

**Highpower:** Hey, Horace, those curlers are going to be picked up...

**Singlemind:** Then we have no problem. No pickup, no order.

**Highpower:** What are you doin', punishing me because the pickup was delayed a little?

**Singlemind:** If I wanted to punish you I wouldn't even see you, Highpower.

**Highpower:** Well, you want this deal and all of a sudden you come on with this hangup about the curlers.

**Singlemind:** You can call it a hangup or whatever the hell you like, but you'll pick up those damn curlers by the end of the week or I'll discontinue every one of your products as fast as I can ship 'em back to you.

**Highpower:** Don't get hot under the collar, Singlemind... This is a two-way street, you know, you don't do us a big fat favor makin' money off our line...

## ANALYSIS: WHAT PROBLEM?
### Selling a Product for Resale

**Script Theme:** "Climb the highest mountain."

**Tapes:** Parent—"Knock 'em dead." "You'll never make it."

Child —"Just watch me." "I forgot to empty the garbage."

**Key Crossed Transaction:**

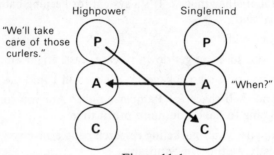

Figure 11.1

**Ulterior Message:** "The magic doesn't work."

**Basic Life Position:** "I'm not-OK—you're OK"; covered up by: "I'm OK—you're not-OK."

**Games:** *Punish Me, Psychiatry*

**Roles:** Victim ("I've got something hot...")

Persecutor ("We'll take care of those curlers.")

Obviously Prescott Highpower is excited. It is his business to be excited, i.e., to have something hot. That's how he has learned to be a successful salesman and "Climb the highest mountain."

Other areas of his work do not interest him so much because they do not satisfy his stroke hunger. Picking up unsold items like the 156 dozen disposable hair curlers does nothing for his Child ego state. Since his Child is his greatest strength in selling, he tends to discount the Adult, and along with that, information concerning how the less dramatic needs of his client are to be met.

The action builds slowly with an apparently OK set of transactions leading to a mutually satisfactory conclusion. But the real energy is somewhere else. It is in Singlemind's Parent, who is fed up with the unsalable order, and in Highpower's Child, eager to make the next sale. So the game ensues between an angry Parent and an overly eager Child (Fig. 11.2).

The information which Prescott Highpower is confronted with about the load of hair curlers cannot be brushed aside, not if the new sale is going to be made. That is clear at the beginning. But Highpower does not see it as a problem to be solved. Rather, he becomes defensive about the loss—"Everybody has a bomb once in a while." That response is directed not to the need of his client but to the threat of the

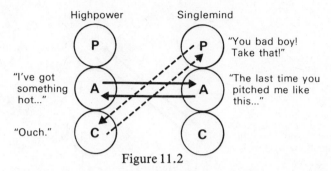

Figure 11.2

Parent. He is probably responding more to the Parent in his own head than to his client's Parent. He just wants to get out from under the threat of its blaming and put-downs, and get on with the next try to make it big. With all his energy caught up in fending off his Critical Parent, he does not have enough left to see that Singlemind is really in his Adult, seeking information about when the problem will be solved. Highpower responds with his Parent, using its protective side to fend off what appears to be an attack from Singlemind.

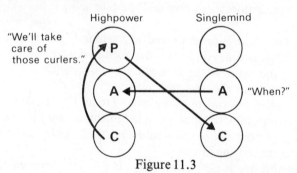

Figure 11.3

Though his response comes across Parent, it originates in the scared, threatened Child, which then uses the Parent like a mask.

The buyer, Horace Singlemind, has no useful point of contact offered to him by Highpower. His request for information and his problem have been discounted. The feelings that go with his being discounted will be cashed in later.

Highpower pushes ahead with his Child, having seemingly escaped the power of the critical Parent (Fig. 11.4). He has forced Singlemind to respond in only one way—to his Child. That response comes across with a low level of interest or commitment. Singlemind is indulging a demanding child and has not much patience.

In the time frame set by Singlemind, there is no time to get the facts across. The flash cards convey vital information which is lost until, at a later time, it is punitively called for in the Critical Parent statement "And I suppose your marketing research people gave you the word that the public is breathlessly waiting for SaniBaby?" Here is the harassed Parent responding. Not really listening, Singlemind has already decided that he just wants to get this over with as soon as possible, and get the problem

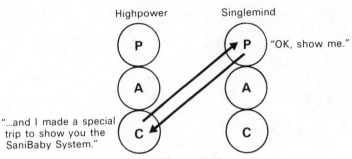

Figure 11.4

solved *his* way. The problem for him is not the purchase of the SaniBaby System, but the return of the disposable hair curlers. And, since Highpower's Adult is not plugged in, none of this information about his client registers at all. Instead, he still ploughs ahead as if everything were fine, ignoring all the warning signals.

Singlemind, the buyer, doesn't want a sales pitch. He is just getting an incidental matter out of the way with an old hand who tends to talk too much. Yet Highpower presses on with the "great floorstand prepack" despite being told "skip the rest of those cards."

Unfortunately, his Child is programmed to "selling," not responding to the obvious realities of the situation. His pitch is designed to control the response of the buyer, not to explore the issues in the here and now. Consequently, when the real problem confronts him, he is shocked and confused.

The "guaranteed sale" appears to be the closure to his Child, but it is not. When the real problem confronts him, it appears as a judgment against him, but again, it is not. Being defensive, he does not see the real issue at all—only the Critical Parent which he puts on the face of the buyer.

The game of *Punish Me* is now under way. It is a war between Highpower's not-OK kid and what he perceives to be the Critical Parent of Singlemind.

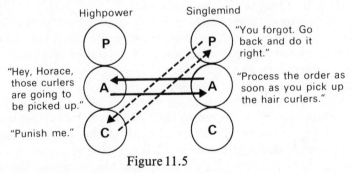

Figure 11.5

Highpower feels punished, unfairly. An old Child tape is triggered, and he slips out of the here and now to fight an old battle, for a cause that was long since lost. Actually, Singlemind is a little fed up with Highpower's misplaced exuberance and his lack of contact with the real problem. But that rather slight impatience triggers a much greater response in Highpower's Child. He has been trying so hard to please the Parent and now he meets rejection. His feeling is compounded. Not only is it a rejection of his sales pitch, but moreover it feels like a rejection of his entire self. In his early life experience that would have been catastrophic because his very survival depended on the real Parent.

Singlemind is not interested in the issue of punishment. He wants a problem solved. That is why he has seen Highpower. He does not want to get involved in a discussion about psychological motivation either. He wants results, and the game Highpower is into doesn't provide that.

Highpower again uses his Parent to protect his Child with the remark about the "hangup."

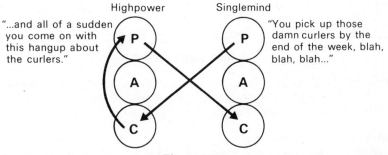

Figure 11.6

"All of a sudden" it is, at least to his scared Child ego state, because Highpower has not been listening to the point that Singlemind has repeatedly made. He uses his Parent to defend his Child by attacking Singlemind's motives.

His Child is using a punitive game as a defense. His game of *Psychiatry* is a variation on *Now I've Got You*. Its hidden message is: "You've got a psychological problem and are not facing reality." In this case the reality is that a sale has been made and the matter of the curlers will be taken care of in due time. But, clearly, Highpower's perception of reality is very different from Singlemind's. Highpower is influenced by his impatient Child and Singlemind by his impatient Parent.

Finally, Highpower gets even tougher in the next crossed transaction.

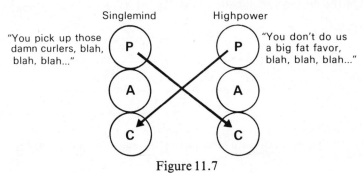

Figure 11.7

His magic is not working. Is there any solution? Surely not at the rate things are going. Things can only get worse as the game proceeds from a first degree game, which ends up in bad feelings, to a second degree game, which ends up in a broken relationship—in this case a lost customer. Highpower, caught up in the dynamics of a Parent that is protecting a hurt Child by attacking the buyer personally, is left with no awareness of the problem or the buyer's perception of the situation. There is just no energy left for his Adult.

Knowing these things, how could you transform this disaster into a success? Clearly Highpower has gone wide of his mark. Not only has he missed the sale, but he is nowhere near stimulating action to get resale. Would it have been possible at all for him in that situation to get the Desired Result, or should he have revised his strategy entirely, based on the feedback?

### Awareness Format

Revise the script by writing your own version of this dialogue, which has ended so badly. Use the Awareness Format to do it, and then compare your version with ours. A sample for the Awareness Format is provided in the appendix.

#### I. Tapes
Change Highpower's Child tape ("Just watch me." "I forgot to empty the garbage.") into an Adult statement.

Adult: _____

_____

Change Highpower's Parent tape ("Knock 'em dead." "You'll never make it.") into an Adult statement.

Adult: _____

_____

#### II. Key Crossed Transaction
Change the crossed transaction (see Fig. 11.1) to make it complementary.

Highpower: _____

_____

Singlemind: _____

_____

#### III. Ulterior Message
Change Highpower's Ulterior Message ("The magic doesn't work.") into an Adult statement.

Adult: _____

_____

## IV. Role

Change what Highpower said in his Victim/Persecutor role to an Adult statement.

Victim: "I've got something hot..."

Persecutor: "We'll take care of those curlers."

Adult: _____

_____

## V. Style

On a scale from 1 to 10 grade the applicability of each criterion from Highpower's point of view. (See the introduction to this book for a detailed explanation of the criteria.)

A. A Developmental style may be effective:

Grade<br>1 to 10

  1. The Adult is available in the other person. _____

  2. A joint decision is important. _____

  3. An impasse has been reached and a new approach is desired. _____

  4. There is time for study and discussion. _____

B. A Controlling style may be effective:

  1. The chief priority is to get the task done as soon as possible. _____

  2. You intend to direct the project in your own way. _____

  3. Ready assent is forthcoming from the other person's Child. _____

  4. Negotiation is futile, and you control all the alternatives. _____

C. A Relinquishing style may be effective:

  1. The other person has relevant information which you do not possess. _____

  2. The other person's Child is upset and needs your Nurturing Parent. _____

  3. Development of the other person's autonomy is the most important objective. _____

  4. The other person is autonomous, yet a caring relationship still exists. _____

D. A Defensive style may be effective:

  1. Your Child is confused or frustrated. _____

  2. Participation is against the moral standards of your Parent. _____

3. Your support is not required. _____

4. You are aware that games are being played. _____

Fill in the criteria score chart below according to the numbers indicated for each style. Use the criteria score chart to select a transactional style which is designed to effectively achieve Highpower's Desired Result.

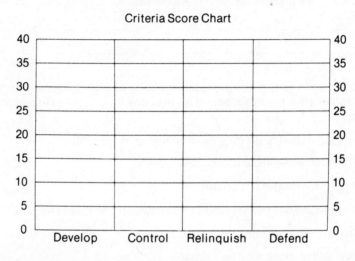

Criteria Score Chart

If another style is graded close to the highest one on your chart, you may want to incorporate that in your approach. Both may be appropriate at different times in the dialogue or discussion.

*Strategy*

1. What style is indicated for the Improved Dialogue? _____

_____

2. Make some notes on how Highpower's strategy might be improved, using the style indicated.

_____

_____

_____

_____

_____

_____

_____

_____

_____

_____

_____

Now read the Improved Dialogue and compare it with what you have written in Sections I through V.


## THE IMPROVED DIALOGUE
### Selling a Product for Resale

**Highpower:** Horace, how are you? Good to see you... Looks like you're busy as always... (*Laughs*)

**Singlemind:** (*Perfunctorily grabs Highpower's hand, gestures him to a seat*) Hi.

**Highpower:** You know I've got your regular order in the works, Horace, and I want to thank you for giving me this extra time to make a presentation on our new product... and I tell you it is a money-maker!

**Singlemind:** Okay, Press, but listen, I really have just five minutes so give it to me straight and fast.

**Highpower:** You know me, Horace, I don't fool around. When I've got something hot I don't waste a lot of time with preliminaries, I get right to it and when I tell you you ought to have space in your stores for a hot one, man you know I'm telling it like it is!

**Singlemind:** The last time you pitched me like this I bought a load of disposable hair curlers. You haven't picked 'em up yet. Why don't you issue the credit up front?... Let's see... (*Shuffles papers*) I've got 156 dozen to return.

**Highpower:** I'm getting a message, Horace. Those things get picked up or I'm doing my act for nothing, right?

**Singlemind:** I think you've got it.

**Highpower:** I'll tell it to you straight, Horace. The OK for that pickup has gotten hung up in our office procedures... I know it'll be OK'd because that whole line is being discontinued. But let me make one suggestion before we pull those curlers—one that might pay off for you.

**Singlemind:** I'll listen, but if it means you're going to stick me with those curlers, get ready to duck!

**Highpower:** No, no way you get stuck. Look, the TV ads on those curlers ran until about two weeks ago... The name is still recognizable and there is some demand. Why not take the whole 156 dozen and put them in a couple of dumps... I'll get the display units and set them up for you... and run them out at say 10% over cost? You build the discount image, maybe pick up a few bucks... and whatever doesn't move in two weeks, I guarantee will be picked up immediately or we'll issue credit for 'em! What do you say? It's a way to get me out of that paper shuffling routine at the home office and for you to get some mileage out of the stuff.

**Singlemind:** Press, I don't know why I'm doing this... But you've been pretty straight over the years and that's a legit copout... I'll let you get away with it. I'll give you a couple of store locations to put that stuff in and you get it out by the end of the week, right?

**Highpower:** Right. And thanks... Now I've got three minutes left to show you SaniBaby—a money maker if you ever saw one.

**Singlemind:** Don't do the whole routine, Press... Give me the meat.

**Highpower:** OK, I've got this flashcard presentation... Can I set this stand up on your desk?

**Singlemind:** No, don't set any damn stand on my desk. You have all that info in a brochure or something I can read later?

**Highpower:** Sure...

**Singlemind:** OK, show me the package and cut the story to essentials.

**Highpower:** Here it is...

**Singlemind:** That's pretty damn big...

**Highpower:** You found shelf space for Pampers, right? Are you sorry? Matter of fact, for starters—we don't need shelf space at all!

**Singlemind:** Oh?

**Highpower:** Here, look, this is a four dozen floor stand prepack... Carries a full 50% margin and a three dollar handling allowance *plus* a three dollar ad allowance.

**Singlemind:** Great, if it sells. You haven't told me what the hell it is... Looks like a diaper holder...

**Highpower:** SaniBaby is a system for keeping babies dry, with terrific market potential... The research is all in that brochure... And the repeat sale buildup is terrific...

**Singlemind:** Refills, huh?

**Highpower:** You get right down to cases. Right. And the refills take up a lot less room than Pampers—and show you a better margin. The TV push starts in four weeks...

**Singlemind:** Guaranteed sale, right?

**Highpower:** Right. I see it as three prepacks for each A store and two each for the B's... You'll want to arrange for planogram shelf space once you see how it moves.

**Singlemind:** Write the order for two prepacks for each A store and one for each B.

**Highpower:** Good enough, and thanks, Horace.

**Singlemind:** And if you don't take care of those curlers like we agreed I'll shove them and these glorified diapers up your happy nose! (*Laughs*) Get outa here!

## Awareness Format Applied to Your Own Situation

### I. Background
Describe briefly a situation in which you have had a responsible part and are not satisfied with the results:

_____

_____

_____

### II. Desired Result
What was your Desired Result? _____

_____

### III. Key Crossed Transaction
In that situation identify a key crossed transaction in which the response came from the Parent or the Child in the other person.

What you said: _____

_____

The response: _____

_____

Diagram your crossed transaction:

### IV. Tapes
Imagine yourself as you were when you were a very young child and think of an experience which is similar to the one you have just described. Be aware of the people who appear in your mind's eye, what you felt and what you were trying to say to them.

In the recent situation which you have just described, what appears to be the Child tape influencing your behavior from that old scene in your past?

Child tape: _____

_____

Change your Child tape into an Adult statement:

Adult: _____

_____

What appears to be your Parent tape? If you need to, go back to the memory you just retrieved for an awareness of that tape.

Parent tape: _____

_____

Change your Parent tape into an Adult statement:

Adult: _____

_____

## V. Ulterior Message

What Ulterior Message did you send to the other person? You can spot your Ulterior Message by examining your Parent and Child tapes to see how they exerted a negative influence on your transactional style in that situation.

Your Ulterior Message: _____

_____

## VI. Basic Life Position

Check out your feelings in that situation. What Basic Life Position do they seem to indicate?

Check one: ☐ I'm not-OK—you're OK.
            ☐ I'm not-OK—you're not-OK.
            ☐ I'm OK—you're not-OK.
            ☐ I'm OK—you're OK.

What is the feeling? _____

## VII. Game Awareness

Now you can see how the parts of your game fall into place. Write here your Desired Result (see II above).

_____

Write here your Ulterior Message (see V above).

_____

Write here the response you got in the crossed transaction (see III above).

_____

Write here your Basic Life Position in that situation (see VI above) and the feeling that goes with it.

Basic Life Position:_____

Feeling:  _____

What game seems to be indicated here?

Name:  _____

To get out of that game, change your Ulterior Message in that game into an Adult statement.

Adult:  _____

_____

## VIII.  Role

What role were you playing in that game? Check one:

☐ Persecutor   ☐ Victim   ☐ Rescuer

Describe what you said or did to play that role.

_____

_____

Change that to an Adult behavior or statement:

Adult:  _____

_____

## IX.  Style

On a scale from 1 to 10 grade the applicability of each criterion from your point of view. (See the introduction to this book for a detailed explanation of the criteria.)

Grade
1 to 10

A. A Developmental style may be effective:

1. The Adult is available in the other person.          _____

2. A joint decision is important.          _____

3. An impasse has been reached and a new approach is desired.          _____

4. There is time for study and discussion.          _____

B. A Controlling style may be effective:

   1. The chief priority is to get the task done as soon as possible. _____

   2. You intend to direct the project in your own way. _____

   3. Ready assent is forthcoming from the other person's Child. _____

   4. Negotiation is futile, and you control all the alternatives. _____

C. A Relinquishing style may be effective:

   1. The other person has relevant information which you do not possess. _____

   2. The other person's Child is upset and needs your Nurturing Parent. _____

   3. Development of the other person's autonomy is the most important objective. _____

   4. The other person is autonomous, yet a caring relationship still exists. _____

D. A Defensive style may be effective:

   1. Your Child is confused or frustrated. _____

   2. Participation is against the moral standards of your Parent. _____

   3. Your support is not required. _____

   4. You are aware that games are being played. _____

Fill in the criteria score chart below, Use the criteria score chart to develop a transactional strategy that will effectively attain your Desired Result.

Criteria Score Chart

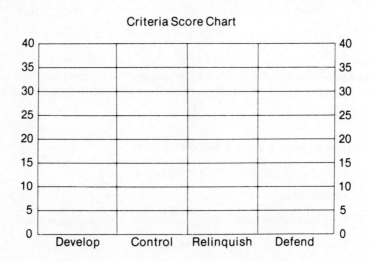

If some other style appears to be close to another one on your chart, you may want to incorporate that in your approach. Both may be appropriate at different times in the dialogue or discussion.

*Strategy*

1. What style is indicated for your Improved Dialogue?

_____

2. Look over carefully what you have written in Sections I-IX and use it to help yourself decide how to implement that style. Then make some notes on what you will do:

_____

_____

_____

_____

_____

_____

_____

_____

3. When will you do it? _____

_____

# CHAPTER TWELVE

# Will it throw up on my shoes?

**Subject:** Selling a product for end use
**Initiator:** Salesman
**Point of View:** Salesman
**Desired Result:** Make the sale
**Salesman:** Robert Grasemoyl     **Buyer:** Andre Vamonos

Robert Grasemoyl has set up his new copying machine in Andre Vamonos's office for a selling demonstration.

**Robert:** Now then, before I go ahead with the demonstration, let me ask you a few questions, Mr. Vamonos.

**Andre:** How do you turn the thing on?

**Robert:** I'll be showing you all of that in just a few minutes... How many copies do you make a month, Mr. Vamonos?

**Andre:** I don't know. Hundred... maybe two... will that thing copy color?

**Robert:** The Ultracopier will do anything that is needed in the way of office copying, Mr. Vamonos... of course, it doesn't copy *in* color...

**Andre:** I know that. Start it up.

**Robert:** I'll do a full demonstration for you in a moment... we don't want to just make copies, do we? I mean, that machine serves a purpose in your business framework...

**Andre:** Yeah. It makes copies. Or does it take stenography too?

**Robert:** (*Laughs*) You do have a sense of humor, Mr. Vamonos. I appreciate that. Now, assuming you make two hundred copies a month, is that an average really or do you have some heavier months and some lighter?

**Andre:** I guess about even... I don't keep track... my secretary would know...

**Robert:** I see. Would you like to call her in?

**Andre:** No.

**Robert:** Oh. Uh... well... on the basis of two hundred separate copies each month, this model of the Ultracopier would be ideal and as matter of fact for the same base monthly cost you could make as many as five hundred copies.

**Andre:** Terrific. I probably won't need five hundred, so will that mean I pay for the equivalent of five hundred copies each month even if I make just a hundred?

**Robert:** Oh, no... compared to any other copier on the market the first two hundred will cost less per copy and five hundred, which you won't need as you say, could cost even less. So if you rescheduled your copying procedures...

**Andre:** I don't even know if the machine can produce *one* copy, much less hundreds. Do you plan to get it working or do you plan only to tell me about it and let me guess if it can work?

**Robert:** I am sorry, Mr. Vamonos, I just wanted to get some details out of the way... Let's get right to the machine... Notice that this model is in a beige. It can be had in sixteen colors of your choice—red, blue, magenta, pistachio...

**Andre:** Fine. Don't give me the whole menu. Start it.

**Robert:** This is the paper length control, notice it is marked from 5 inches to 15 inches, right here on the side in clear calibrations...

**Andre:** I noticed that real quick... I'm really a very alert fellow.

**Robert:** (*Laugh*) There's that wonderful sense of humor again... Now, the controls are so simple that it's almost impossible to make a mistake in using the machine.

**Andre:** Good—then let me try it.

**Robert:** Just give me something you would like copied, Mr. Vamonos, and I'll show you how to get the best service out of the Ultracopier.

**Andre:** Doesn't it have instructions?

**Robert:** Printed right on that panel there...

**Andre:** Well, then get out of the way and I'll see if I like the way it works...

**Robert:** No, we just aren't supposed to do it that way... I have to explain the workings of the Ultracopier as I work it for you and make the first copy...

**Andre:** Why?

**Robert:** Because... Well, we want our customers to feel secure about the reliability of the Ultracopier...

**Andre:** Are you telling me that if I turn it on it'll bite me or throw up on my shoes?

**Robert:** Of course not, I mean that's the starter switch there, if you want to be the one to push it, go right ahead, I really don't care.

**Andre:** Neither do I. The machine I have now is working perfectly well. Why don't we forget the whole thing?

**Robert:** But...


## ANALYSIS: NO, NO, NOT YET!
### Selling a Product for End Use

**Script Theme:** "Be perfect."

**Tapes:** Parent—"Do as I say."
　　　　Child—"Have your way, I don't care."

**Key Crossed Transaction:** See Fig. 12.1.

**Ulterior Message:** "Do it my way."

**Basic Life Position:** "I'm OK—you're not-OK."

**Game:** *Not Just Now*

**Role:** Rescuer ("I'll be showing you all that in a few minutes...")

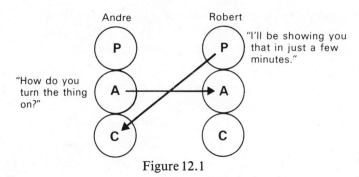

Figure 12.1

Robert Grasemoyl, the salesman, has a Parent that programs him to try hard and do it right. His Parent is not unkind. Rather, it is very nurturing. It is just out of touch with the here and now. It discounts Andre's Adult request for information and spunky Child interest in the machine. If Andre's Child behaved the way Robert's did, everything would be fine. But Andre's Child is not programmed to wait patiently for his turn. If Robert's Adult were turned on, he would read the signals he is getting and respond to where the energy is activated in the buyer. The fact that the machine is all set up in the office is probably the single most powerful message. But instead of letting the machine speak for itself, Robert goes after statistical information which Andre does not have.

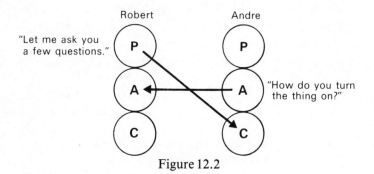

Figure 12.2

Robert now has his first clue, which he misses. Andre wants to see the machine work. But Robert, instead of responding to that cue, goes with the program taped into his head by sales training. Unfortunately, he is acting as if he had the power to control the buyer, which he does not. His response to the buyer's request is a put-down, again from his Parent (Fig. 12.3).

They have arrived at an impasse. They are speaking past each other. Andre wants basic information about the machine. Robert stubbornly intends to set up his sales pitch. Encountering this wall of China, Andre goes into his Rebellious Child.

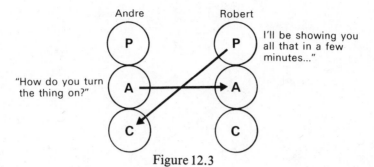

Figure 12.3

It is clear that Andre is not interested in giving information about office operations, but there is some Child curiosity about what the machine might do: "... Will that thing copy color?" This bit of wondering is dealt with firmly by Robert's Parent: "The Ultracopier will do anything that is needed in the way of office copying..."

In this response the seller's Parent is again putting down the buyer's Child, which is the very element he needs most to make the sale.

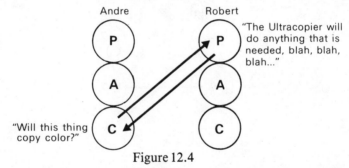

Figure 12.4

In most instances Robert would probably do well using his pitch, with the way his machine can save costs in the office operation. That would make a fine appeal to the Parent of the average buyer. But Andre is simply not there. He moves between Adult and Child, neither of which is getting satisfied by Robert.

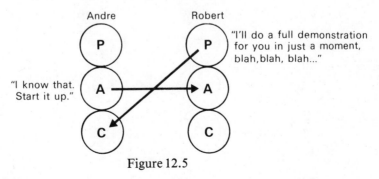

Figure 12.5

Andre is not used to such treatment. He is getting exasperated. So his energy goes into his Rebellious Child, which takes some pot shots at Robert's ponderous approach.

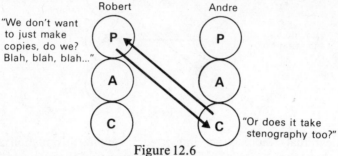

Figure 12.6

And still the button is unpushed! There stands Andre's Child eagerly waiting and Robert's Parent is saying, "No, no, not yet!"

Robert then asks for more information, which is not available. He is programmed to make a hard pitch on how the machine could save money. But Andre's Parent isn't interested, and his Child is getting desperate.

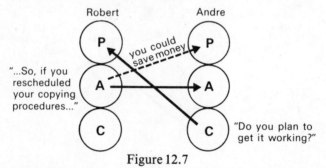

Figure 12.7

Precious moments are being lost. The option to hook the buyer's Child is long since gone by and the seller, who is only on page 2 of the training manual, still has a way to go. His Parent is blandly unaware of the havoc he is producing in the buyer's Child, who is being tantalized beyond endurance.

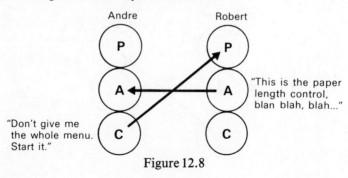

Figure 12.8

By this time what may have been Andre's impish humor has now turned to sarcasm. But Robert's bemused Parent does not detect it. His Parent is just being tolerant of a slight deviation from the usual norm in a proper sales presentation. Little does he know that the kid he has stifled has a verbal sling shot, and a very good aim.

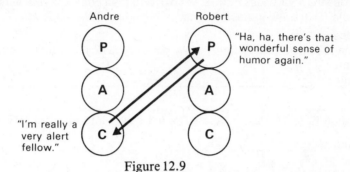

Figure 12.9

And so it goes. More delay. The seconds seem like hours to the buyer's Child. Why would this particular buyer ever want to use the machine anyway—other than for the fun of it? But no, he must wait until the seller gets to page 3 of the training manual. Andre makes a last-ditch effort to use his Adult and see how the thing works.

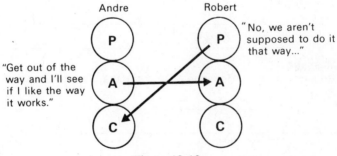

Figure 12.10

By now, to Andre's Child the enticing fun machine has turned into a monster, which might bite or throw up on his shoes. Robert has discounted once too often. The thrill is gone and so is the sale. When permission to push the button is finally granted it is too late.

Knowing these things, how would you now make the sale if you were Robert Grasemoyl?

---

## Awareness Format

Revise the script by writing your own version of this dialogue, which has ended so badly. Use the Awareness Format to do it, and then compare your version with ours. A sample for the Awareness Format is provided in the appendix.

**I. Tapes**

Change Robert's Child tape ("Have your way, I don't care.") into an Adult statement.

Adult: _____

_____

Change Robert's Parent tape ("Do as I say.") into an Adult statement.

Adult: _____

_____

**II. Key Crossed Transaction**

Change the crossed transaction (see Fig. 12.1) to make it complementary.

Robert: _____

_____

Andre: _____

_____

**III. Ulterior Message**

Change Robert's Ulterior Message ("Do it my way.") into an Adult statement.

Adult: _____

_____

**IV. Role**

Change what Robert said in his Rescuer role to an Adult statement.
Rescuer: "I'll be showing you all that in a few minutes..."

Adult: _____

_____

_____

**V. Style**

On a scale from 1 to 10 grade the applicability of each criterion from Robert's point of view. (See the introduction to this book for a detailed explanation of the criteria.)

A. A Developmental style may be effective:

Grade<br>1 to 10

   1. The Adult is available in the other person. _____

   2. A joint decision is important. _____

   3. An impasse has been reached and a new approach is desired. _____

   4. There is time for study and discussion. _____

B. A Controlling style may be effective:

   1. The chief priority is to get the task done as soon as possible. _____

   2. You intend to direct the project in your own way. _____

   3. Ready assent is forthcoming from the other person's Child. _____

   4. Negotiation is futile, and you control all the alternatives. _____

C. A Relinquishing style may be effective:

   1. The other person has relevant information which you do not possess. _____

   2. The other person's Child is upset and needs your Nurturing Parent. _____

   3. Development of the other person's autonomy is the most important objective. _____

   4. The other person is autonomous, yet a caring relationship still exists. _____

D. A Defensive style may be effective:

   1. Your Child is confused or frustrated. _____

   2. Participation is against the moral standards of your Parent. _____

   3. Your support is not required. _____

   4. You are aware that games are being played. _____

Fill in the criteria score chart below according to the numbers indicated for each style. Use the criteria score chart to select a transactional style which is designed to effectively achieve Robert's Desired Result.

If another style is graded close to the highest one on your chart, you may want to incorporate that in your approach. Both may be appropriate at different times in the dialogue or discussion.

Criteria Score Chart

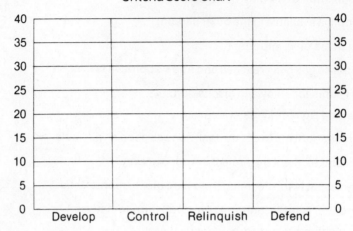

*Strategy*

1. What style is indicated for the Improved Dialogue? _____

_____

2. Make some notes on how Robert's strategy might be improved, using the style indicated.

_____

_____

_____

_____

_____

_____

_____

_____

_____

Now read the Improved Dialogue and compare it with what you have written in Sections I through V.

## THE IMPROVED DIALOGUE
### Selling a Product for End Use

In any book offering advice on human actions and reactions, the authors tend to come from the Parent time and again and sometimes make up their own little games. We're quite aware in this instance, for example, that we're handing down a Parental rebuke and indulging in the game of *Shoulda Done It Different* (on a non-Transactional level) when we say that Robert Grasemoyl had no business showing up with the machine ready to operate before he had the information about Andre Vamonos's needs available to him. This could have been obtained in any number of ways—a mailed questionnaire, a phone interview, a previous call without the machine, etc. Robert showed up unarmed to take advantage of the Child-oriented excitement the operating machine would generate.

With that out of the way, we can turn to the legitimate, Adult-originated advice and guidance this situation calls for. (Since the authors have been established as experts in the subject at hand, the Adult instructions that are presented lose their Parental colorations. Right?)

Let's see how Robert Grasemoyl might handle the situation if he is fully aware of the TA dynamics that are at work. . .

**Robert:** I've got the machine set up and ready to use, Mr. Vamonos. Would you like to see it work before we discuss how it can be of value to you in your business?

**Andre:** Good idea.

**Robert:** Fine. Now, is there something you'd like me to copy for you? A piece of literature or a letter. . .

**Andre:** Didn't you bring anything along that you could demonstrate with?

**Robert:** Sure. I just wanted to give you the opportunity to run something of your own through the machine. Here. . . Let's start with this photograph. . .

**Andre:** Photograph? Will that thing copy half tones?

**Robert:** Why don't you try it yourself and see? Here. . . The photo goes on the table area here. . . Come on, you can run it.

**Andre:** Lemme see. . . Ah, you set the length here, right?

**Robert:** Exactly.

**Andre:** And then. . . just push this button. . . there! Hey, this isn't a bad copy! Can this thing handle colored originals?

**Robert:** It can. . . Of course you get black and white copies. . . (*Laugh*)

**Andre:** (*Laugh*) I understand.

**Robert:** But it will pick up any color. At the rate of one copy every half-second, by the way—automatically.

**Andre:** Sounds terrific. . . But I have the feeling it goes way beyond my budget. . . I mean, I've got this Happicopi machine that costs me just a nickel a copy. . .

**Robert:** The Ultracopier can cost less than that. Much less—just depends on one thing.

**Andre:** The down payment?

**Robert:** Nope. The number of copies you make per month.

**Andre:** Well... it isn't really a hell of a lot...

**Robert:** I think you might be pleasantly surprised. Here, you wanted to check on color... Why don't you run through a couple of these brochures you have here?

**Andre:** OK... Let's see... Boy that thing does do a good job, I must admit. Too bad I can't...

**Robert:** Would you guess you make three copies a day?

**Andre:** I don't really know exactly—but it's more than three.

**Robert:** Four? Five?

**Andre:** Probably around eight or ten I think, maybe a couple more.

**Robert:** That would put you over two hundred copies a month. At that level, you could have this machine and the cost would be 4.8¢ per copy. If it ran as high as four hundred copies, you bring it down to 4¢.

All through this part of the conversation, Andre is playing with the demonstrator.

**Andre:** If that's correct, Mr.—(*Looks at his business card again*) Mr. Grasemoyl, I think we can make a deal.

**Robert:** Did you like the beige color or would you prefer your machine in apricot or...

A note here. What has been done is to make Andre's Child an ally instead of a petulant adversary. The Child is so hooked by the marvelous toy that it supplies the Adult with information intended to verify the possibility of owning one. It is quite likely that Andre's copying needs are somewhat smaller than the figures fed to the Adult by the happy Child... but the sale is made. We have made no allowance for the possibility that the Ultracopier demonstrator might break down during the demonstration; barring that eventuality, however, it should be possible to have this dialogue work out just as we have said. This underlines an important point: in business as well as in personal exchanges, it is by no means always necessary nor indeed desirable to have a totally Adult-Adult contact.

---

## Awareness Format Applied to Your Own Situation

### I. Background
Describe briefly a situation in which you have had a responsible part and are not satisfied with the results:

_____

_____

_____

### II. Desired Result
What was your Desired Result? _____

_____

### III. Key Crossed Transaction
In that situation identify a key crossed transaction in which the response came from the Parent or the Child in the other person.

What you said: _____

_____

The response: _____

_____

Diagram your crossed transaction:

### IV. Tapes
Imagine yourself as you were when you were a very young child and think of an experience which is similar to the one you have just described. Be aware of the people who appear in your mind's eye, what you felt and what you were trying to say to them.

In the recent situation which you have just described, what appears to be the Child tape influencing your behavior from that old scene in your past?

Child tape: _____

_____

Change your Child tape into an Adult statement:

Adult: _____

_____

What appears to be your Parent tape? If you need to, go back to the memory you just retrieved for an awareness of that tape.

Parent tape: _____

_____

Change your Parent tape into an Adult statement:

Adult: _____

_____

## V. Ulterior Message

What Ulterior Message did you send to the other person? You can spot your Ulterior Message by examining your Parent and Child tapes to see how they exerted a negative influence on your transactional style in that situation.

Your Ulterior Message: _____

_____

## VI. Basic Life Position

Check out your feelings in that situation. What Basic Life Position do they seem to indicate?

Check one: ☐ I'm not-OK—you're OK.
           ☐ I'm not-OK—you're not-OK.
           ☐ I'm OK—you're not-OK.
           ☐ I'm OK—you're OK.

What is the feeling? _____

## VII. Game Awareness

Now you can see how the parts of your game fall into place. Write here your Desired Result (see II above).

_____

Write here your Ulterior Message (see V above).

_____

Write here the response you got in the crossed transaction (see III above).

_____

Write here your Basic Life Position in that situation (see VI above) and the feeling that goes with it.

Basic Life Position: _____

Feeling: _____

What game seems to be indicated here?

Name: _____

To get out of that game, change your Ulterior Message in that game into an Adult statement.

Adult: _____

_____

## VIII. Role

What role were you playing in that game? Check one:

☐ Persecutor    ☐ Victim    ☐ Rescuer

Describe what you said or did to play that role.

_____

_____

Change that to an Adult behavior or statement:

Adult: _____

_____

## IX. Style

On a scale from 1 to 10 grade the applicability of each criterion from your point of view. (See the introduction to this book for a detailed explanation of the criteria.)

Grade
1 to 10

A. A Developmental style may be effective:

1. The Adult is available in the other person.    _____

2. A joint decision is important.    _____

3. An impasse has been reached and a new approach is desired.    _____

4. There is time for study and discussion.    _____

B. A Controlling style may be effective:

    1. The chief priority is to get the task done as soon as possible. _____

    2. You intend to direct the project in your own way. _____

    3. Ready assent is forthcoming from the other person's Child. _____

    4. Negotiation is futile, and you control all the alternatives. _____

C. A Relinquishing style may be effective:

    1. The other person has relevant information which you do not possess. _____

    2. The other person's Child is upset and needs your Nurturing Parent. _____

    3. Development of the other person's autonomy is the most important objective. _____

    4. The other person is autonomous, yet a caring relationship still exists. _____

D. A Defensive style may be effective:

    1. Your Child is confused or frustrated. _____

    2. Participation is against the moral standards of your Parent. _____

    3. Your support is not required. _____

    4. You are aware that games are being played. _____

Fill in the criteria score chart below, Use the criteria score chart to develop a transactional strategy that will effectively attain your Desired Result.

Criteria Score Chart

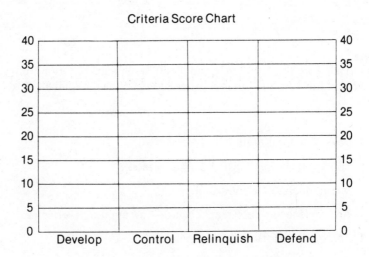

If some other style appears to be close to another one on your chart, you may want to incorporate that in your approach. Both may be appropriate at different times in the dialogue or discussion.

*Strategy*

1. What style is indicated for your Improved Dialogue?

_____

2. Look over carefully what you have written in Sections I-IX and use it to help yourself decide how to implement that style. Then make some notes on what you will do:

_____

_____

_____

_____

_____

_____

_____

_____

_____

_____

_____

3. When will you do it?  _____

_____

# Miscellaneous

# CHAPTER THIRTEEN

# My kid has got these red bumps...

**Subject:** Customer complaint, product or service
**Initiator:** Customer
**Point of View:** Executive taking complaint
**Desired Result:** Satisfy complainant while maintaining good will and
protecting company interests
**Customer:** Mary Alice Mommasan    **Company executive:** James Cortley

Cortley is the brand manager for SaniBaby Systems and an irate phone call has been turned over to him.

**James:** Good afternoon, my name is Cortley, may I help you?

**Mary:** Are you the president of SaniBaby Company?

**James:** No, I'm the brand manager for the Systems, though, and I'd...

**Mary:** I told that stupid girl I wanted to talk to the president of the company and not some flunky...

**James:** Ma'am, I'm the equivalent of the president for this particular brand and I'd be delighted to be of service to you.

**Mary:** I'll bet! Well, if I can't get to the brass, I guess you'll have to do. You lousy big companies never really give a damn about the little people out here who buy those things you put all over TV, do you?

**James:** Oh, but we care...

**Mary:** Then why won't the president talk to me? Maybe he's busy counting his money, huh?

**James:** I...

**Mary:** Never mind. My baby is sick and what are you going to do about it?

**James:** I'm sorry the child is ill... But what do you expect...

**Mary:** It was that SaniBaby System that did it!

**James:** Now, just a minute, ma'am, the SaniBaby System cannot cause any child to...

**Mary:** Waddya mean, cannot? You telling me that I'm off my nut or something? My kid has got these red bumps on his rear and everywhere like that...

**James:** We can't prevent diaper rash in all the babies in the world...

**Mary:** Boy, you are a wise one, mister! It's more than a plain diaper rash... Don't you think a mother would recognize a diaper rash?... It's an infection and your SaniBaby System caused it...

**James:** Look, lady, you're making an accusation that can't be true. The SaniBaby refills are totally sterile and...

**Mary:** Yeah, I guess, the first time you use them. But what about after you dry one out and use it again?

**James:** You did what?

**Mary:** I dried them out and got two or three uses out of each refill before I threw them away... With the high prices you charge...

**James:** Those refills are intended to be used just once. Lady, you...

**Mary:** Really, wise guy? Where does it say that in the instructions? Huh? Where? It tells you how to clip in the refill and how to take it out but it sure doesn't say not to use it again...

**James:** Well, anyone of reasonable intelligence should realize that if the things are marked disposable...

**Mary:** Now I'm not reasonable or intelligent, huh?

**James:** Ma'am, we accepted this collect call from Dubuque to be of service, but apparently I can't satisfy you over the phone... Why don't you write our...

**Mary:** I'll write. I'll write to the FDA, the FTC, the Nader guys and all the papers.

**James:** Well, if that's the way you feel about it, go ahead and write all you like... I was about to offer to...

**Mary:** To what? What were you about to offer?

**James:** I would have been delighted to send you a gross of SaniBaby refills with a letter of full instructions but...

**Mary:** But what? Afraid it would cost you too much?

**James:** Look, we don't buckle under to threats here, lady.

**Mary:** Threats, huh? OK, then... wait till you see the letters I write... I got lots of time to write letters and SaniBaby isn't the only product you make! There are a few things I could say about those disposable hair curlers too... and boy is everybody gonna read about it!


## ANALYSIS: NO CONTACT AT ALL
### Customer Complaint, Product or Service

**Script Theme:** "Mea culpa." ("It's all my fault.")

**Tapes:** Parent—"Be nice."

Child —"I want you to love me (and you never will)."

**Key Crossed Transactions:** See Figs. 13.1 and 13.2.

**Ulterior Message:** "You are too stupid to talk to."

**Basic Life Position:** "I'm not-OK—you're not-OK."

**Game:** *We Aim to Please*

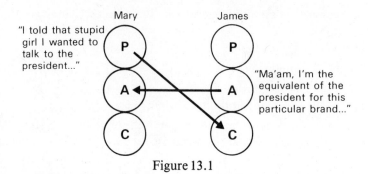

Figure 13.1

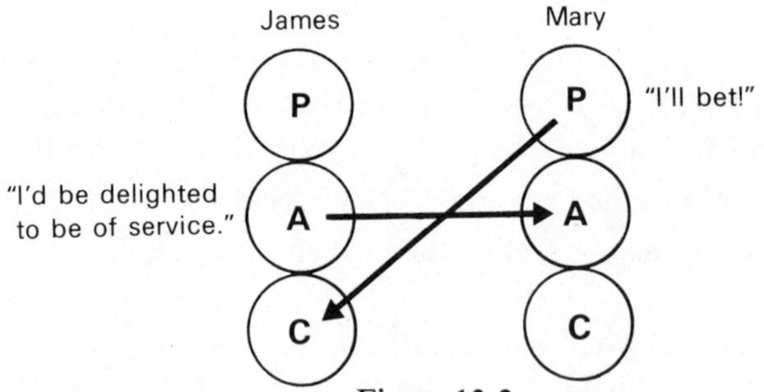

Figure 13.2

**Roles:** Persecutor ("Well, anyone of reasonable intelligence...")
Rescuer ("Oh, but we care...")
Victim ("...we don't buckle under to threats...")

This is one dialogue which perhaps should not have taken place at all. What is a brand manager doing talking to such an irrational complainer? Yet, she might do the company some harm, and in the interests of good public relations, perhaps it is worth his time and trouble. However, since what Mr. James Cortley is dealing with is the irrational Critical Parent, nothing he will ever do will satisfy her complaints, and indeed the harm done may be greater as a result of his efforts.

There must be something in James that allows for this. He has some inner penchant for the kind of strokes he is getting in this dialogue. His Parent programs him to be polite to the customers, and yet at the same time looks down its nose at them, and his Child takes abuse. Somehow he has to prove that he can be polite no matter how badly he is treated. The negative strokes he gets affirm his Basic Life Position that other people are not-OK and neither is he. He tries hard to have it otherwise through his long suffering, patient Nurturing Parent. Yet in the end that's the way it turns out. Over and over again he gets nowhere.

In reading this dialogue, on one level it seems hilarious, and yet on another it is sad because it depicts such a disastrous waste of time for the people involved.

No positive results occur. There is only a tremendous amount of strong feeling. The reason for that is that the only thing happening is a game. Games unfortunately trigger in us a kind of wicked glee. However, if we are involved in them ourselves, the final feeling is negative. Both the customer and the brand manager in this dialogue end up unsatisfied.

James's Child has already decided before the game begins that he is not-OK and neither are customers. His game only proves that once again it is so. As previously indicated, it reaffirms his Basic Life Position. The game he plays is encouraged by his Parent tapes; and his Adult is not aware that he is playing a game.

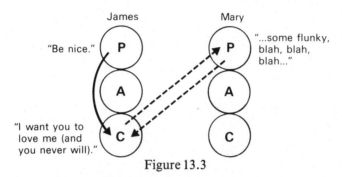

Figure 13.3

Obviously the customer is heavily into games also, and their games match up so both can get the kind of strokes from the exchange that will fit their scripts.

Though James could easily spot Mary's game, it would not be useful to call it to her attention because she is not aware of it. What would help James is to discover his own propensity toward games and to make a conscious effort to change.

In the opening of the dialogue James does stay in his Adult, despite the put-downs of the customer. However, his phrase, ''I'd be delighted to be of service to you'' is a dead giveaway to the angry Mary. She now has her mark: a willing victim.

Perhaps his phrase is just a polite mode of expression; but if critically examined it is saying that to some extent he will be pleased to take abuse from her. Though neither of them is analyzing what is going on, both of them respond to what is coming across. Mary has already been abusive, and James is now being unduly polite. Mary's game is so powerful that James has little opportunity to respond. But she is not interested in anything more than an object on which to vent her wrath, anyhow.

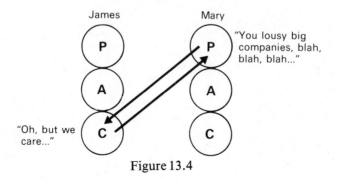

Figure 13.4

In this game, the manager taking the complaint is apparently saying, "We're here to be of service." However, in a hidden way he is coming across with a conviction that customers are stupid. The response he gets from the customer fits the hidden message and in the end he feels frustrated and hurt.

Putting himself in the position of the patient listener who hands over the initiative to the other person, James does not get any chance to use his Adult because Mary does not address his Adult.

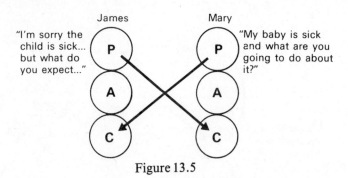

Figure 13.5

Here we have an attempt to placate and a counteraccusation. The transactions are crossed, and both parties are at an impasse. James is not aware that there is no appeasement for the Critical Parent. No way is Mary interested in problem solving. She is out to dump bad feelings collected over a long period of time—at least as far back as the last time she bought hair curlers.

The conversation now turns into a duel between two Parent ego states—each aiming for the weakness in the Child of the other.

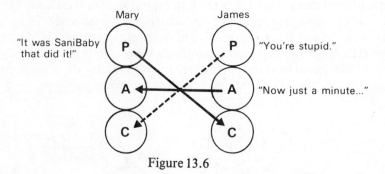

Figure 13.6

James has the good manners to cover his Critical Parent with a veneer of politeness. But Mary's Child knows what's going on. She is more direct. She does not have any concerns about maintaining good relations and can afford to play a second degree game. He cannot. Still she gets the message and responds to it.

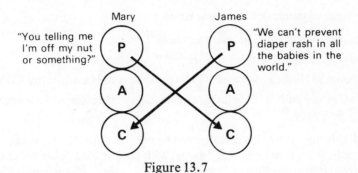

Figure 13.7

Each Child ego state is getting negative strokes; each Parent is handing them out. At this point the game is a perfectly working mechanism for a stroke economy which flows around the Adult like this:

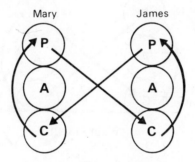

Figure 13.8

It is a closed system. The hurt Child uses the Parent to attack and hurt the other Child, which then does the same, and on and on it goes.

The game climax occurs when Mary's stupidity becomes obvious to him, through her reference to reusing the disposable refills.

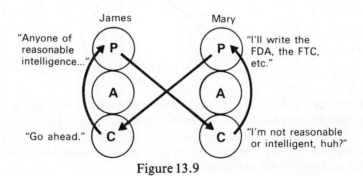

Figure 13.9

The basic dynamics of the game are:

1. Apparent Message: "We aim to please."

2. Hidden Message: "You're too stupid."

3. Response to Hidden Message: "Your product is to blame for my kid being sick."

4. Payoff at the end: Bad feelings, and an angry customer set to wage a campaign attacking SaniBaby.

In all this mad flurry it's a little hard to tell just what *is* happening analytically. But basically, it's a complementary game, with each person going around the drama triangle from Persecutor to Rescuer to Victim. In reality, they are both Victims of the Critical Parent who persecutes the Rescuer until it fails.

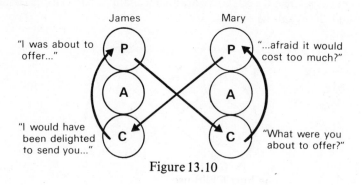

Figure 13.10

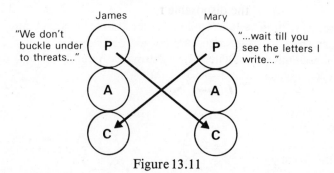

Figure 13.11

In the end, all the energy centers in their Critical Parents and everybody loses.

Is there any way out of this, other than hysterical laughter? In a situation of this kind, James would perhaps do well to use caution and protect himself with his Adult by staying out of it all together. To do that he must leave his negative Basic Life Position and accept the fact that he's OK.

## Awareness Format

Revise the script by writing your own version of this dialogue, which has ended so badly. Use the Awareness Format to do it, and then compare your version with ours. A sample for the Awareness Format is provided in the appendix.

### I. Tapes
Change James's Child tape ("I want you to love me (and you never will).") into an Adult statement.

Adult: _____

_____

Change James's Parent tape ("Be nice.") into an Adult statement.
Adult: _____

_____

### II. Key Crossed Transactions
Change the crossed transactions (see Figs. 13.1 and 13.2) to make them complementary.

Mary:_____

_____

James: _____

_____

Mary:_____

_____

James: _____

_____

### III. Ulterior Message
Change James's Ulterior Message ("You are too stupid to talk to.") into an Adult statement.
Adult: _____

_____

### IV. Role
Change what James said in his Persecutor/Rescuer/Victim role to an Adult statement.
Persecutor: "Well, anyone of reasonable intelligence..."
Rescuer: "Oh, but we care..."
Victim: "...we don't buckle under to threats..."

Adult: _____

_____

## V. Style

On a scale from 1 to 10 grade the applicability of each criterion from James's point of view. (See the introduction to this book for a detailed explanation of the criteria.)

Grade
1 to 10

A. A Developmental style may be effective:

   1. The Adult is available in the other person. _____

   2. A joint decision is important. _____

   3. An impasse has been reached and a new approach is desired. _____

   4. There is time for study and discussion. _____

B. A Controlling style may be effective:

   1. The chief priority is to get the task done as soon as possible. _____

   2. You intend to direct the project in your own way. _____

   3. Ready assent is forthcoming from the other person's Child. _____

   4. Negotiation is futile, and you control all the alternatives. _____

C. A Relinquishing style may be effective:

   1. The other person has relevant information which you do not possess. _____

   2. The other person's Child is upset and needs your Nurturing Parent. _____

   3. Development of the other person's autonomy is the most important objective. _____

   4. The other person is autonomous, yet a caring relationship still exists. _____

D. A Defensive style may be effective:

   1. Your Child is confused or frustrated. _____

   2. Participation is against the moral standards of your Parent. _____

   3. Your support is not required. _____

   4. You are aware that games are being played. _____

Fill in the criteria score chart below according to the numbers indicated for each style. Use the criteria score chart to select a transactional style which is designed to effectively achieve James's Desired Result.

Criteria Score Chart

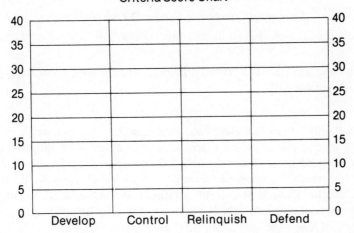

40 —                                                                    — 40
35 —                                                                    — 35
30 —                                                                    — 30
25 —                                                                    — 25
20 —                                                                    — 20
15 —                                                                    — 15
10 —                                                                    — 10
 5 —                                                                    —  5
 0 —                                                                    —  0
      Develop      Control     Relinquish      Defend

If another style is graded close to the highest one on your chart, you may want to incorporate that in your approach. Both may be appropriate at different times in the dialogue or discussion.

*Strategy*

1. What style is indicated for the Improved Dialogue? _____

_____

2. Make some notes on how James's strategy might be improved, using the style indicated.

_____

_____

_____

_____

_____

_____

_____

_____

_____

Now read the Improved Dialogue and compare it with what you have written in Sections I through V.

## THE IMPROVED DIALOGUE
### Customer Complaint, Product or Service

There is the obvious temptation to handle this transaction in a rather peremptory manner...

**Secretary:** We have a collect call from Dubuque, Mr. Cortley, complaining about SaniBaby. Shall I accept it?

**James:** No.

This would certainly avoid the ridiculous conversation that we have witnessed. Unfortunately, the company for which James Cortley works has a policy of talking to any consumer complainants. Since that policy does exist, we are faced—or James is faced—with this irate, unreasonable female. Can TA help James through this experience? Can the Desired Result be attained? At the risk of assuming the appearance and sound of a particularly bad soap opera, let us see if the TA-trained James Cortley can make the best of a pitiful encounter...

**James:** Good afternoon, my name is Cortley, may I help you?

**Mary:** Are you the president of SaniBaby Company?

**James:** Yes.

(We have rather rather swiftly avoided a whole series of crossed transactions and taken away a serious irritant from the female's Parent by this minor distortion of fact. As brand manager, he is, in fact, the equivalent of the president of *that brand*. Why get involved in explanations?)

**Mary:** Well. Well, my baby is sick and what are you going to do about it?

**James:** I'm going to listen sympathetically while you tell me just what your baby's problem is.

**Mary:** I don't need your damn sympathy, it was that SaniBaby System that did it!

**James:** You know, if one of my kids was sick and I thought I knew who caused it, I'd really blow my top too... so I can understand why you used that language... I assume you're not that kind of person, Mrs. Mommasan...

**Mary:** Don't you patronize me, Mr. President! My kid has got these red bumps on his rear and everywhere like that and it was the SaniBaby System that did it...

**James:** I see. How?

**Mary:** Well, it... there was somethin' in it that made the kid get infected...

**James:** The refills are packed in airtight sterile condition. Was the package opened before you used it?

**Mary:** Well, of course, when I used 'em for the second time after they dried out...

**James:** You used them for the second time... I see. Well... uh, it's possible they lost their sterility while they were hung out drying.

**Mary:** Oh?

**James:** Yes, you see they should be used only once and thrown away.

**Mary:** At the prices you get? Listen, the directions don't say that nowhere.

**James:** You might not have noticed, ma'am, but disposal directions are given on the box. In any case, we do care about your baby, ma'am, and as an obviously concerned mother you will certainly have the child checked by a physician. . . It's possible that there was some other cause for those red bumps.

**Mary:** Well, and who is going to pay for. . .

**James:** As a gesture of good faith, since you made a human error in using the SaniBaby refills, we will send you a case free.

**Mary:** Oh, and what about. . .

**James:** My secretary will take your name and address so that the shipment can be made.

**Mary:** Well, I. . .

**James:** Thank you for your call. Goodbye.


We have done several things in this rather ideally concluded version of the dialogue. We have removed an important irritant (the presidency) and we have avoided sticking needles in Mary's rather sensitive Child ego state that previously filled the Parent with overflowing venom. In addition, we have quite bluntly bribed her greedy Adult. The combination would probably work. If at any point, however, this Mommasan became once again overly obnoxious, TA, pragmatism and good sense would dictate that the conversation be ended by placing the receiver upon its cradle without comment and awaiting the lady's letters (if they came) to be handled by the legal department.

## Awareness Format Applied to Your Own Situation

### I. Background
Describe briefly a situation in which you have had a responsible part and are not satisfied with the results:

_____

_____

_____

### II. Desired Result
What was your Desired Result? _____

_____

### III. Key Crossed Transaction
In that situation identify a key crossed transaction in which the response came from the Parent or the Child in the other person.

What you said: _____

_____

The response: _____

_____

Diagram your crossed transaction:

### IV. Tapes
Imagine yourself as you were when you were a very young child and think of an experience which is similar to the one you have just described. Be aware of the people who appear in your mind's eye, what you felt and what you were trying to say to them.

In the recent situation which you have just described, what appears to be the Child tape influencing your behavior from that old scene in your past?

Child tape: _____

_____

Change your Child tape into an Adult statement:

Adult: _____

_____

What appears to be your Parent tape? If you need to, go back to the memory you just retrieved for an awareness of that tape.

Parent tape: _____

_____

Change your Parent tape into an Adult statement:

Adult: _____

_____

## V.  Ulterior Message

What Ulterior Message did you send to the other person? You can spot your Ulterior Message by examining your Parent and Child tapes to see how they exerted a negative influence on your transactional style in that situation.

Your Ulterior Message: _____

_____

## VI.  Basic Life Position

Check out your feelings in that situation. What Basic Life Position do they seem to indicate?

Check one:  ☐ I'm not-OK—you're OK.
　　　　　　☐ I'm not-OK—you're not-OK.
　　　　　　☐ I'm OK—you're not-OK.
　　　　　　☐ I'm OK—you're OK.

What is the feeling? _____

## VII.  Game Awareness

Now you can see how the parts of your game fall into place. Write here your Desired Result (see II above).

_____

Write here your Ulterior Message (see V above).

_____

Write here the response you got in the crossed transaction (see III above).

_____

Write here your Basic Life Position in that situation (see VI above) and the feeling that goes with it.

Basic Life Position:_____

Feeling: _____

What game seems to be indicated here?

Name: _____

To get out of that game, change your Ulterior Message in that game into an Adult statement.

Adult: _____

_____

## VIII. Role

What role were you playing in that game? Check one:

☐ Persecutor   ☐ Victim   ☐ Rescuer

Describe what you said or did to play that role.

_____

_____

Change that to an Adult behavior or statement:

Adult: _____

_____

## IX. Style

On a scale from 1 to 10 grade the applicability of each criterion from your point of view. (See the introduction to this book for a detailed explanation of the criteria.)

Grade
1 to 10

A. A Developmental style may be effective:

1. The Adult is available in the other person. _____

2. A joint decision is important. _____

3. An impasse has been reached and a new approach is desired. _____

4. There is time for study and discussion. _____

B. A Controlling style may be effective:

1. The chief priority is to get the task done as soon as possible.  _____

2. You intend to direct the project in your own way.  _____

3. Ready assent is forthcoming from the other person's Child.  _____

4. Negotiation is futile, and you control all the alternatives.  _____

C. A Relinquishing style may be effective:

1. The other person has relevant information which you do not possess.  _____

2. The other person's Child is upset and needs your Nurturing Parent.  _____

3. Development of the other person's autonomy is the most important objective.  _____

4. The other person is autonomous, yet a caring relationship still exists.  _____

D. A Defensive style may be effective:

1. Your Child is confused or frustrated.  _____

2. Participation is against the moral standards of your Parent.  _____

3. Your support is not required.  _____

4. You are aware that games are being played.  _____

Fill in the criteria score chart below, Use the criteria score chart to develop a transactional strategy that will effectively attain your Desired Result.

Criteria Score Chart

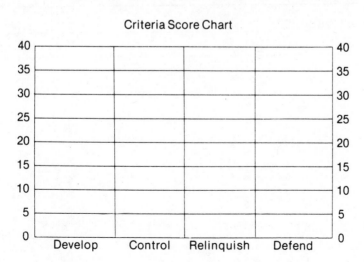

If some other style appears to be close to another one on your chart, you may want to incorporate that in your approach. Both may be appropriate at different times in the dialogue or discussion.

*Strategy*

1. What style is indicated for your Improved Dialogue?

_____

2. Look over carefully what you have written in Sections I-IX and use it to help yourself decide how to implement that style. Then make some notes on what you will do:

_____

_____

_____

_____

_____

_____

_____

_____

_____

_____

3. When will you do it? _____

_____

# CHAPTER FOURTEEN

# I'm not trying to step on your toes…

**Subject:** Employee complaint other than salary
**Initiator:** Employee
**Point of View:** Employer
**Desired Result:** Satisfy complainant while maintaining company policies
            and employee morale
**Employee:** Larry Garrett     **Employer:** Kurt Trumpeter

Larry Garrett is a foreman at the National Products Co. Kurt Trumpeter is a personnel department junior executive. Larry has come into Kurt's office and is seated opposite him.

**Kurt:** Your note requesting this interview indicated you had a problem, Larry. Why don't we get right to it?

**Larry:** OK, look—I don't want it to look like I'm one of those guys who's always looking for more authority or anything...

**Kurt:** I think your authority is pretty well outlined in the company manual. That shouldn't present any problem...

**Larry:** Well, hell, saying that you make it kind of tough to tell you what's on my mind.

**Kurt:** By all means, feel free to say whatever you want to. If we can do what you want, according to company rules, we will... If we can't, well, that's the way the cookie crumbles, right? (*Laughs*)

**Larry:** Yeah, I guess. Look, as foreman I have charge of a team of twelve people...

**Kurt:** Right. And my records indicate you're handling it well.

**Larry:** Well, I've got to keep the respect and... loyalty... of those people to the company, and the way I do that is through me...

**Kurt:** We like to think that at least a good part of the loyalty you speak of comes from basic company policies, Larry... I mean, we don't want to make the whole operation a question of individual personalities...

**Larry:** OK, fine, so it's company policies that we'll talk about.

**Kurt:** Those policies have been worked out over many years, and we feel that they are among the most enlightened...

**Larry:** For crying out loud, I'm not trying to overturn the whole business, Kurt... Give me a chance to tell you what's on my mind.

**Kurt:** Sure, sure. Don't let this thing get emotional... We're adults and we can discuss this on an adult level...

**Larry:** Sorry... I didn't mean to sound belligerent or anything... Look, to make it short, all I want is the right to allow someone on my team to leave early if I feel they have a good reason.

**Kurt:** You have that authority now, I believe.

**Larry:** Well, yeah, but not really... I have to make a report of...

**Kurt:** Are you objecting to the report? I mean, it isn't that big a job...

**Larry:** It isn't the making of the report that bugs me.

**Kurt:** Well, then, I guess there isn't any problem.

**Larry:** There sure is! Listen, after I make that report, it goes to personnel...

**Kurt:** Certainly. That's part of our function...

**Larry:** I'm not trying to step on your toes, Trumpeter...

**Kurt:** I should hope not!

**Larry:** Darn it... You guys hold onto those reports for weeks...

**Kurt:** So what?

**Larry:** So my people don't know if they're getting paid for that time off until you make a decision.

**Kurt:** Well, we certainly have to determine if the time off is valid...

**Larry:** That's the point. As foreman, I think I ought to have enough weight with the company so that if I say it's OK, it's OK... I mean, I'm not talking about days off, I'm just talking about a matter of a couple of hours at the most...

**Kurt:** Now, think about this, Larry. We have over 800 employees, and if every one of them was allowed to take a couple of hours off...

**Larry:** For crying out loud, I'm not planning to furlough the whole organization. I'm talking about special situations...

**Kurt:** And our job in personnel is to verify that those situations are truly special.

**Larry:** And take two weeks to a month to do it!

**Kurt:** How many of those situations have we rejected recently?

**Larry:** I don't know for sure...

**Kurt:** When you have a complaint, don't you think you ought to have all the facts handy?

**Larry:** It doesn't matter! It's the not knowing that bugs my team...

**Kurt:** Sorry, but some things have to stay in line with policy and this is one of them.

**Larry:** All right, I guess the only thing to do is go through channels...

**Kurt:** I'm glad you understand that.

**Larry:** I'll take it up with the shop steward. I guess a formal complaint is the only way. Goodbye. Thanks.

## ANALYSIS: YOU DON'T HAVE THE FACTS
### Employee Complaint Other Than Salary

**Script Theme:** "Follow the rules."

**Tapes:** Parent—"Do as I say."

Child —"I want to be a good boy."

**Key Crossed Transaction:**

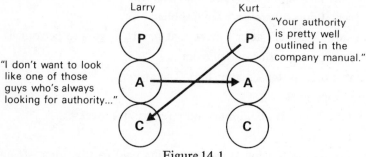

Figure 14.1

**Ulterior Message:** "The book counts, you don't."

**Basic Life Position:** "I'm OK—you're not-OK."

**Game:** *Company*

**Role:** Persecutor ("When you have a complaint, don't you think you ought to have all the facts handy?")

Rescuer ("If we can do what you want, according to company rules, we will...")


Kurt Trumpeter exhibits the kind of behavior that would please higher-ups. He keeps tight control according to company policies. Yet he misses his Desired Result. He is very wide of the mark. Operating almost entirely in his Parent, he has little or no way to be sensitive to the particular concerns of his employee, Larry. The Parent ego state is not tuned in to the here and now, and so his transactional style does nothing for the problem or the morale of the employee. He misses the opportunity to develop his employee and to build any kind of real relationship with him. In the end the problem is still there, compounded by the fact that the employee feels discounted.

At the end of the session Kurt probably feels safe; but that is only because he is unaware of the reaction he has produced in Larry. Such ignorance is bliss but it is a fool's paradise.

Early in the session Kurt makes it perfectly clear that he is operating from his Parent ego state: "I think your authority is pretty well outlined..." "...according to company rules..." "That's the way the cookie crumbles..." These are all Parent statements, impersonal, rule-oriented and unrelated to the here-and-now situation.

Larry works hard to get his problem across, but there is no Adult available in Kurt.

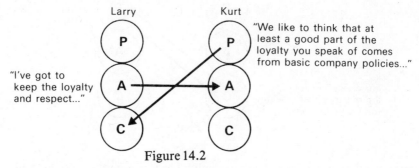

Figure 14.2

He is now into the second crossed transaction. The first was indicative of how the entire interview would proceed.

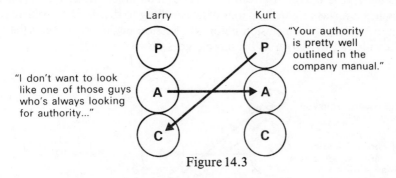

Figure 14.3

And it does. It stays in the same vein throughout. With all Larry's efforts to get him to see the problem, Kurt never does get out of his Parent.

Larry even tries to uncross the transactions by meeting Kurt on his own ground: "OK, fine, so it's company policies that we'll talk about." But this is too much. Stroking Kurt's Parent is the last thing he needs. It just makes him revel in it all the more: "Those policies have been worked out over many years, blah, blah, blah..." is his proud Parent response.

Kurt, by staying in his Parent ego state, does not leave any opening for Larry to come across with the information. Though he says he's adult, he doesn't have an open mind. He is really just going on a Parent tape that says "Don't be emotional" (Fig. 14.4).

The reality of the situation is that Larry is indeed dealing with an issue of authority. He is seeking to reaffirm a power which he believes is rightfully his, and which has been taken away. Kurt, being in his Parent, intends to retain control and not give any of it away. The reports still have to be made and Personnel still must

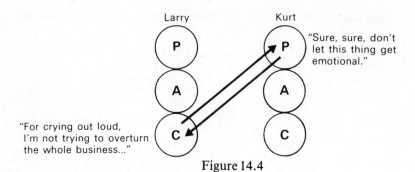

Figure 14.4

decide if the permission to leave was valid. He does not relinquish his authority and so the commitment, morale and motivation of his employee will suffer. Larry is too spunky to let it go at that, however.

The game Kurt is playing is from his Parent. The hidden message is that the company policy is always right. Apparently he is willing to discuss the problem; but the decision is a foregone conclusion before the session begins. In the end the bad feelings are collected by Larry, as his morale goes down.

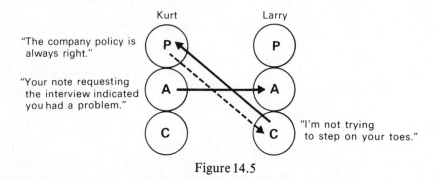

Figure 14.5

The game moves subtly, but powerfully, through their conversation, controlling the action. Risk is scary to Kurt's Child ego state and the game provides a kind of morbid security from his Parent. Of course, that kind of overprotectiveness prevents Kurt from developing also. The seeming Rescuer is really a persecutor not only to subordinates but to himself as well. The true nature of that Parent comes out when he attacks Larry with the question: "How many of those situations have we rejected lately?" The question is designed to embarrass and hurt, and it finds its mark; but it really is a coverup for Kurt's unwillingness to part with power at any cost. Personnel officers will be fair despite being misunderstood, *and they will retain control.*

He sends the zinger home with "When you have a complaint, don't you think you ought to have all the facts handy?" The benign Rescuer has clearly become the wicked

Persecutor. Perhaps he really does feel that Larry is stepping on his toes. At any rate, the Victim he was there to help and is now attacking will be saving up some feeling to cash in when he talks to the shop steward. He will have a lot of dirty stamps in his collection by that time. And the prize may be how he gets back at Kurt. If the shop steward doesn't give a hang about company rules, there may be a new Victim in the story.

If you were Kurt and aware of these things, how would you use your Adult to get in touch with Larry's OKness and really communicate, instead of playing games?

---

### Awareness Format

Revise the script by writing your own version of this dialogue, which has ended so badly. Use the Awareness Format to do it, and then compare your version with ours. A sample for the Awareness Format is provided in the appendix.

**I. Tapes**

Change Kurt's Child tape ("I want to be a good boy.") into an Adult statement.

Adult: _____

_____

Change Kurt's Parent tape ("Do as I say.") into an Adult statement.

Adult: _____

_____

**II. Key Crossed Transaction**

Change the crossed transaction (see Fig. 14.1) to make it complementary.

Kurt: _____

_____

Larry: _____

_____

**III. Ulterior Message**

Change Kurt's Ulterior Message ("The book counts, you don't.") into an Adult statement.

Adult: _____

_____

**IV. Role**

Change what Kurt said in his Persecutor/Rescuer role to an Adult statement.
Persecutor: "When you have a complaint, don't you think you ought to have all the facts handy?"

Rescuer: "If we can do what you want, according to company rules, we will..."

Adult: _____

_____

## V. Style

On a scale from 1 to 10 grade the applicability of each criterion from Kurt's point of view. (See the introduction to this book for a detailed explanation of the criteria.)

Grade
1 to 10

A. A Developmental style may be effective:

1. The Adult is available in the other person. _____

2. A joint decision is important. _____

3. An impasse has been reached and a new approach is desired. _____

4. There is time for study and discussion. _____

B. A Controlling style may be effective:

1. The chief priority is to get the task done as soon as possible. _____

2. You intend to direct the project in your own way. _____

3. Ready assent is forthcoming from the other person's Child. _____

4. Negotiation is futile, and you control all the alternatives. _____

C. A Relinquishing style may be effective:

1. The other person has relevant information which you do not possess. _____

2. The other person's Child is upset and needs your Nurturing Parent. _____

3. Development of the other person's autonomy is the most important objective. _____

4. The other person is autonomous, yet a caring relationship still exists. _____

D. A Defensive style may be effective:

1. Your Child is confused or frustrated. _____

2. Participation is against the moral standards of your Parent. _____

3. Your support is not required. _____

4. You are aware that games are being played. _____

Fill in the criteria score chart below according to the numbers indicated for each style. Use the criteria score chart to select a transactional style which is designed to effectively achieve Kurt's Desired Result.

Criteria Score Chart

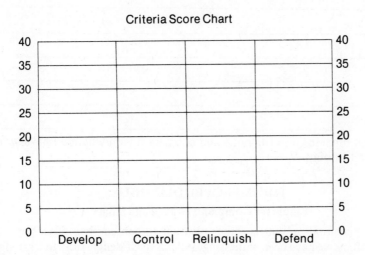

If another style is graded close to the highest one on your chart, you may want to incorporate that in your approach. Both may be appropriate at different times in the dialogue or discussion.

*Strategy*

1. What style is indicated for the Improved Dialogue? _____

_____

2. Make some notes on how Kurt's strategy might be improved, using the style indicated.

_____

_____

_____

_____

_____

_____

_____

_____

_____

_____

_____

_____

Now read the Improved Dialogue and compare it with what you have written in Sections I through V.

## THE IMPROVED DIALOGUE
### Employee Complaint Other Than Salary

Here we have a situation that is rather pleasant to contemplate after some of the dreadful conflicts we have been witnessing. It lends itself delightfully to a satisfactory conclusion by the direct application of TA principles. With Kurt Trumpeter transactionally aware, he enters the dialogue with an Adult orientation and receptivity that almost automatically avoids the conflict that had ensued. Thus . . .

**Kurt:** Your note requesting this interview indicated you had a problem, Larry. Why don't we get right to it?

**Larry:** OK, look—I don't want it to look like I'm one of those guys who's always looking for more authority or anything . . .

**Kurt:** No explanation is necessary, Larry. Your record pretty well speaks for itself . . . It's a good one. Feel free to speak your mind.

**Larry:** Look, as foreman, I have charge of a team of twelve people . . .

**Kurt:** Right.

**Larry:** Well, I've got to keep the respect and . . . loyalty . . . of those people to the company and the way I do that is through me . . .

**Kurt:** While we don't try to make the company a sort of personality oriented group, there is no question about the fact that you are their point of contact with corporate authority.

**Larry:** OK, right. And I ought to really represent that authority. I mean, well, the fact is what I'm talking about is that I ought to have the right to allow someone on my team to leave early if I feel they have good reason.

**Kurt:** You have that authority now, I believe.

**Larry:** Well, yeah, but not really, I have to make a report of . . . the time and the reason and like that . . .

**Kurt:** I think I need to ask for more information, Larry. You've never had any problems with paperwork, matter of fact I might say your reports generally are very prompt and complete. Is there a problem?

**Larry:** It's not the report itself... Listen, after I make that report it goes to Personnel...

**Kurt:** Right. That's part of our function.

**Larry:** Darn it... You guys hold onto those reports for weeks...

**Kurt:** Well, yes, that's true, we do sometimes have quite a backlog here.

**Larry:** So my people don't know if they're getting paid for that time off until you make a decision.

**Kurt:** I see. What we're talking about pretty much is the delay in our handling the reports.

**Larry:** And the fact that my word ought to be good enough to clear those pay checks.

**Kurt:** Frankly, I think you're right.

**Larry:** You do?

**Kurt:** Of course. We at Personnel have to stamp OK on those special cases, but aren't you aware that it is your opinion or comment on which that OK is based?

**Larry:** Oh. Well, I've been going by the manual and telling my people that I can't say for sure they'll get the pay until I get your OK.

**Kurt:** Technically, that's true. Actually, until you really goof so badly that management loses faith in you—and I surely don't see that happening—your decision is the one that stands. I'll tell you this, though, I appreciate your attitude about going by the rules in the manual... In a company this big there has to be a solid written procedure... I'm sure you understand that...

**Larry:** Oh, yeah, of course...

**Kurt:** But that doesn't mean that management judgment isn't allowed to function within those rules. You can tell your people that when you approve their leaving early, your decision will stand.

**Larry:** Fine and thanks. About those rules... I don't want my team to get the feeling that we bend 'em, so I'll tell 'em that the procedure stands as it's written and my decision is being accepted... unless one of 'em takes advantage of the situation.

## Awareness Format Applied to Your Own Situation

### I. Background
Describe briefly a situation in which you have had a responsible part and are not satisfied with the results:

_____

_____

_____

### II. Desired Result
What was your Desired Result? _____

_____

### III. Key Crossed Transaction
In that situation identify a key crossed transaction in which the response came from the Parent or the Child in the other person.

What you said: _____

_____

The response: _____

_____

Diagram your crossed transaction:

P    P

A    A

C    C

### IV. Tapes
Imagine yourself as you were when you were a very young child and think of an experience which is similar to the one you have just described. Be aware of the people who appear in your mind's eye, what you felt and what you were trying to say to them.

In the recent situation which you have just described, what appears to be the Child tape influencing your behavior from that old scene in your past?

Child tape: _____

_____

Change your Child tape into an Adult statement:

Adult: _____

_____

What appears to be your Parent tape? If you need to, go back to the memory you just retrieved for an awareness of that tape.

Parent tape: _____

_____

Change your Parent tape into an Adult statement:

Adult: _____

_____

## V. Ulterior Message

What Ulterior Message did you send to the other person? You can spot your Ulterior Message by examining your Parent and Child tapes to see how they exerted a negative influence on your transactional style in that situation.

Your Ulterior Message: _____

_____

## VI. Basic Life Position

Check out your feelings in that situation. What Basic Life Position do they seem to indicate?

Check one: ☐ I'm not-OK—you're OK.
☐ I'm not-OK—you're not-OK.
☐ I'm OK—you're not-OK.
☐ I'm OK—you're OK.

What is the feeling? _____

## VII. Game Awareness

Now you can see how the parts of your game fall into place. Write here your Desired Result (see II above).

_____

Write here your Ulterior Message (see V above).

_____

Write here the response you got in the crossed transaction (see III above).

_____

Write here your Basic Life Position in that situation (see VI above) and the feeling that goes with it.

Basic Life Position: _____

Feeling: _____

What game seems to be indicated here?

Name: _____

To get out of that game, change your Ulterior Message in that game into an Adult statement.

Adult: _____

_____

## VIII. Role

What role were you playing in that game? Check one:

☐ Persecutor    ☐ Victim    ☐ Rescuer

Describe what you said or did to play that role.

_____

_____

Change that to an Adult behavior or statement:

Adult: _____

_____

## IX. Style

On a scale from 1 to 10 grade the applicability of each criterion from your point of view. (See the introduction to this book for a detailed explanation of the criteria.)

Grade
1 to 10

A. A Developmental style may be effective:

1. The Adult is available in the other person.    _____

2. A joint decision is important.    _____

3. An impasse has been reached and a new approach is desired.    _____

4. There is time for study and discussion.    _____

B. A Controlling style may be effective:

1. The chief priority is to get the task done as soon as possible.　＿＿＿＿

2. You intend to direct the project in your own way.　＿＿＿＿

3. Ready assent is forthcoming from the other person's Child.　＿＿＿＿

4. Negotiation is futile, and you control all the alternatives.　＿＿＿＿

C. A Relinquishing style may be effective:

1. The other person has relevant information which you do not possess.　＿＿＿＿

2. The other person's Child is upset and needs your Nurturing Parent.　＿＿＿＿

3. Development of the other person's autonomy is the most important objective.　＿＿＿＿

4. The other person is autonomous, yet a caring relationship still exists.　＿＿＿＿

D. A Defensive style may be effective:

1. Your Child is confused or frustrated.　＿＿＿＿

2. Participation is against the moral standards of your Parent.　＿＿＿＿

3. Your support is not required.　＿＿＿＿

4. You are aware that games are being played.　＿＿＿＿

Fill in the criteria score chart below, Use the criteria score chart to develop a transactional strategy that will effectively attain your Desired Result.

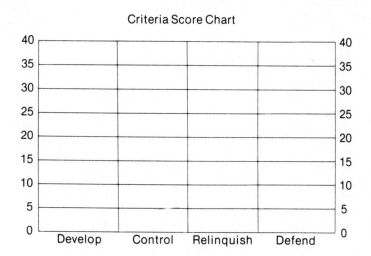

Criteria Score Chart

If some other style appears to be close to another one on your chart, you may want to incorporate that in your approach. Both may be appropriate at different times in the dialogue or discussion.

*Strategy*

1. What style is indicated for your Improved Dialogue?

_____

2. Look over carefully what you have written in Sections I-IX and use it to help yourself decide how to implement that style. Then make some notes on what you will do:

_____

_____

_____

_____

_____

_____

_____

_____

_____

_____

3. When will you do it? _____

_____

# CHAPTER FIFTEEN

# I'm going to ring this little bell...

**Subject:** Problem solving by committee meeting
**Initiator:** Vice President, Marketing
**Point of View:** The company, represented by V.P., Marketing
**Desired Result:** To develop a plan of action to solve a problem
**Participants: V.P., Sales:** Stanley Harvard
                **V.P., Marketing:** Boris Yaleman
                **Agency account executive:** Maria Shtarkfrau
                **Regional sales manager:** Andy Hardknocks
                **Director of trade relations:** Peter Smoothly

The Consumoprod Company manufactures a variety of products, largely based on paper or plastic processing and packaging. Among their strongest concepts is the SaniBaby System. The meeting takes place in the office of Boris Yaleman. He is seated behind his large desk; the other participants are in comfortable chairs in a semicircle facing him and, to some extent, each other.

**Boris:** I guess everybody's here. Does anyone want coffee or anything?... I can have my girl get some...

**Maria:** Some day I'm going to hear an executive say "I'm going to have my *boy* do this or that"... (*Laughs*)

**Boris:** (*Laughs*) I wonder, if my secretary were a man, would I call him "boy"?

**Andy:** Not if he was black! (*General laughter*)

**Peter:** The guy who calls you "boy," Andy, has to be out of his mind or a combination of Muhammed Ali and Larry Czonka!

**Andy:** Being an ex-jock helps me keep that sales force in line! Playin' football has been good for me though...

**Stanley:** Boris, your memo calling this meeting indicated that the subject was to be SaniBaby distribution. I have some figures with me that could give us some clue as to where we stand now.

**Boris:** You bring us right back to the nitty-gritty, Stan. I didn't get any word on that coffee... Anybody?

**Maria:** With cream and sugar...

**Peter:** Can she get some Sanka?

**Stanley:** I'll pass. Can I read these figures while...?

**Boris:** Sure, in a minute, OK? (*On intercom*) Ariadne, get us three coffees and a Sanka... and get some cream and sugar on the side... Hey, Stan, how about a Coke?

**Stanley:** Fine. OK.

**Boris:** And one Coke, Ariadne. Now, while we're waiting for the refreshments I think we can get the meeting rolling...

**Stanley:** Good. Now I have copies of these...

**Boris:** Excuse me, Stanley, but would you permit me to establish the parameters of our session so that we stay right on track, OK? Fine. Above all, we want to keep this discussion on a developmental level, we've had all those solid TA seminars, and we all agree we want to apply what we learned right here and now...

**Peter:** Could I build on that, Boris?

**Boris:** In a few minutes, Peter. Everybody in this room will get the chance to express ideas freely... We don't want the old negatives creeping into our work... Now, if we start to drift into defensive or relinquishing modes or lose our course along the way, I'm going to ring this little bell I have here... (*Rings the bell*)

**Maria:** Whoops, I'm starting to salivate...

**Boris:** You're what?

**Andy:** I guess Maria is identifying with the Pavlovian dogs.

**Maria:** Right on, Andy. (*Andy and Maria laugh*)

**Peter:** Listen, I'm sure Boris didn't intend, I mean Andy wasn't inferring...

**Maria:** It's OK, Peter. I still feel very developmental and my Adult is hanging right in there.

**Stanley:** The figures I have here show that our distribution on SaniBaby is only at 43% in drug outlets while in food we're up to 63%. Now then...

**Boris:** Stanley, you're right, of course, to get us back on track... but don't you think (*Rings bell*) that you're moving into a control mode of expression?

**Stanley:** Yeah, OK, Boris. I wish she'd get here with my damn Coke.

**Andy:** Stan, I think one of our problems is we don't have enough detail people contacting independent drug stores...

**Boris:** Good. We're into the subject at hand. Now then, let me go round the room and ask each of you to make a basic comment on how we can improve distribution on the SaniBaby System in drug outlets.

**Peter:** Shouldn't we have a blackboard or something or hang big sheets of paper on the wall to write these ideas down?

**Andy:** No, that's Creative Problem Solving and we're operating under Transactional Awareness.

**Boris:** That's a good thought... I'll ask Ariadne to...

**Stanley:** She's out getting drinks. I'll take notes, Boris... Let's skip the writing on the wall, OK?

**Peter:** Listen, I read a book recently called *Index Your Mindpower* and they recommend a system where each person in the meeting writes an idea on a 4 x 6 index card. . . it has to be 4 x 6. . . and the index cards are shuffled and each person picks one out. . . it's called Indexomation and the authors prove that several of the largest companies in the country have been able to. . .

**Boris:** I'll look into it, Peter, and if it's worthwhile maybe we can get an Indexomation study group together here. Now, down to cases. Since you have information handy, Stanley, let's start with you. One idea only, right, then we go on to the next person. . .

**Stanley:** Let me provide some basic information before I offer any ideas so that everyone here has a clear picture of the situation. . .

**Boris:** Very well.

**Stanley:** I gave you the distribution figures. . .

**Peter:** What were they again?

**Stanley:** I also passed around printed copies of the data. Peter, you have it right in your hand.

**Peter:** Oh. . . uh—yeah.

**Andy:** 43% drug and 63% food. . .

**Boris:** Don't interrupt, Andy.

**Andy:** I was just giving Peter those figures so that. . .

**Boris:** (*Rings bell*) *Defensive*! Defensive! Come on, Andy, I'm not attacking your motives, I'm just trying to keep this meeting in the developmental quadrant.

**Andy:** Yeah. Right.

**Peter:** I see that we're much weaker in drug than in food.

**Stanley:** It's not quite that simple. It may look that way but in point of fact it's the other way around.

**Peter:** But 63% is a good bit higher than 43%, right? (*Laughs*)

**Maria:** Peter, why don't you shut up and let Stanley finish?

**Boris:** (*Rings bell*) Now, now. I'll have none of that in my office. Peter, that was your Parent crossed with Maria's Child and I think you can both recognize that if we let our transactions get crossed like that we're not going to get anywhere. . .

**Maria:** (*Muttering*) I think I like the index card game better. . .

**Andy:** (Only one who hears Maria—laughs)

**Boris:** What was that, Maria? Speak up, we want to share ideas here not keep them a secret. . . Right?

**Maria:** It wasn't germane.

**Stanley:** Listen, Maria, I realize you're the only woman in the room but I for one don't ever want to have that force you into a relinquishing attitude. . .

**Maria:** Et tu, Stanley?

**Stanley:** What?

**Maria:** Nothing. Regardless of the TA status of our little session, I would really like to hear the information Stanley has for us. The agency has also developed some.

**Boris:** We're really drifting into something I can't even find on my TA chart... I guess you call it crosstalk. Anyhow, I'm going to insist that we get back to an organized procedure.

**Stanley:** OK, then I'll continue...

**Boris:** Please stay on the subject and be brief, Stanley.

**Peter:** How about clearing up that thing about the food distribution problem being worse than the drug... I mean, I don't like to be left looking like some kind of idiot because I think that 63 is bigger than 43...

**Stanley:** Nobody called you an idiot, Peter. It's just that you're not aware...

**Peter:** The hell I'm not! I've established a pretty damn good record in this company!

**Andy:** Hey, Pete, Stan isn't questioning that... Let him finish and you'll see that there isn't anything personal in...

**Boris:** I certainly hope there isn't!

**Stanley:** Dammit, the out-of-stocks in food outlets are running at about 47% and the drug out-of-stocks are only 5%, now how does that grab you, Peter?

**Peter:** If you had given me those statistics to start with I wouldn't have...

**Stanley:** They're all right there on the same sheet with the other figures, so...

**Andy:** Hey, come on, we're on the same team, right?

**Boris:** Well put, Andy! You sound like the old quarterback right there.

**Andy:** I was a defensive tackle and I'm not playing a game.

**Maria:** I sure could use that coffee right about now...

**Boris:** The help you get around here! (*To intercom*) Ariadne! Are you there? Can you get that coffee in here? What? Oh... Hey, sorry folks, the cafeteria's closed... Inventory or something...

**Stanley:** We'll survive. I've got another meeting in twenty minutes---

**Andy:** And there's a guy coming in for an interview...

**Maria:** Look, the agency has worked out a media plan that...

**Peter:** Isn't that a little premature?

**Boris:** (*Ringing bell vigorously*) You're all hooking your angry children! Come on, developmental, huh? Adult and developmental, that's the way...

## ANALYSIS: TRANSACTIONAL ANALYSIS RUNS AMOK
### Problem Solving by Committee Meeting

**Script Theme:** "Good form is what counts."

**Tapes:** Parent—"Always be gracious."

Child—"I get scared when things get out of control."

**Key Crossed Transaction:**

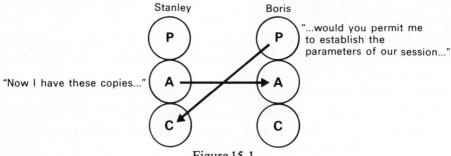

Figure 15.1

**Ulterior Message:** "We're watching for your slipups."

**Basic Life Position:** "I'm OK—You're not-OK."

**Game:** *TA*

**Role:** Persecutor ("I'm going to ring this little bell...")


This scenario depicts what happens when Transactional Analysis itself is used to play games. Like all games, it does not lead to constructive results and, though dramatic—and perhaps even hilarious—in the end it leads to negative feelings.

One moral to this episode is that TA, like all systems for understanding human behavior, is to be used judiciously and with great care. An introduction to TA can provide useful insights, but it does not qualify one to be a TA practitioner. Knowing the names of the pieces does not make one a chess master. To become a TA practitioner requires special training. If Boris at this point in his personal understanding felt the powerful need to run this meeting under strict TA guidelines, he would have been wise to have called in a TA expert to moderate. If his ambition, as it is pointed out later in this analysis, is to be a teacher of TA, he should sign up for extended courses at a good TA institute. In any case, during this scenario, since most of the behavior takes place out of the participants' awareness, it would be extremely difficult for them—Boris included—to discern that process with any degree of objectivity.

This scene, though I found it the most amusing, also has proved to be the most difficult for me to analyze. Not that the analysis itself is difficult to do; rather, I've just found myself avoiding it.

Perhaps that is because it speaks so clearly to the problem of so many of us TA analysts, i.e., the games we play.

Though I have identified with many of the characters in the preceding dialogues, I've begun to realize, as I get into the analysis of this one, that Boris's Parent tapes are very much like my own and it is those tapes which I find it very hard to own, rather than project. Perhaps my co-author had some diabolical intent to lead me to this brink of self-awareness. . . or perhaps he is just an innocent and unusually talented script writer. I will never know. But he has held the mirror up to nature for me and in my analysis of Boris, I know I am looking at myself.

Boris is really conducting a training session, not a meeting. Also, he is acting on the group with no clear group contract. That is to say, they have not agreed to "develop a plan of action." They believe they have come to a meeting called for the purpose of getting information on SaniBaby distribution. The meeting goes nowhere because it does not move according to its announced purpose.

Boris tries to control the meeting and announces that he is being democratic at the same time. Though other ways of structuring time come into play, a meeting can be called for only one of three purposes, as far as the activity or work is concerned:

1. To get information across to others.
2. To receive information from others.
3. To problem-solve.

Of course, it may be a mixture of these, provided the participants understand how and when the agenda is going to change. However, Boris is not acting consistently on any of these purposes. He is having a training session, which would be useful if he were qualified and the others agree. But neither of these conditions is met.

To be in phase, Boris ought not attempt to be a teacher at this meeting since he totally subverts the Desired Result in the abortive attempt. He should be a participant that models a certain kind of behavior. That is, if he were to respond to Stanley's inputs with his Adult listening, that would have more impact on the group than talking *about* those inputs and the possible contributions of others in TA jargon.

Boris has also confused the way he structures time in the session. His pastiming about the refreshments would be OK if were limited to that. However, the pastime intrudes so much on the activity that the work never gets done. The confusion is so great that it isn't clear what's going on—a coffee break or a meeting.

Boris's Child apparently wants everybody to be happy, which would please his Parent, but this interaction goes on to such an extent that the Adult never gets into the act. Also, TA may have provided his Child with a new weapon, albeit a new kind of toy. It may speak to his need to control others as a way of dealing with the threat of the unexpected. His TA game, like all games, not only prevents intimacy but it stifles spontaneity as well. Since nothing new ever happens in a game, it provides a kind of false security by making life predictable.

Boris's TA game goes as shown in Fig. 15.2.

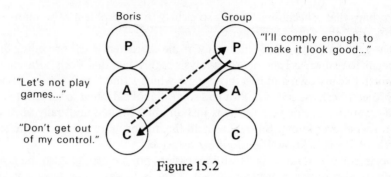

Figure 15.2

Since the group has not accepted his contract to use TA, they quite naturally, though deviously, resist his imposing his will on them. That ends up in anger and frustration.

An alternative to the game for Boris would be a clear contract with the group that they would accept further TA training from him. Of course, that would have to be the motif of a gathering that is entirely separate and distinct from the one we have seen, since the Desired Result would not resemble the one that we have designated and that Boris has called the meeting to accomplish. He would need to study very carefully the Parent, Child and Adult responses he receives to determine the level of seriousness and commitment of the group before making a decision to go ahead with his special TA training sessions. Were he to separate the desire to teach from his function as a catalytic leader in this fashion and attack the problem really facing the group in this session, he could then get out of his attempt at playing Rescuer, which predictably takes him to the Victim role when he is not successful and which finally ends (again predictably) in his attacking the group to give vent to his anger and frustration. Like all Rescuers, he is not prepared to deal with the autonomy of those he is trying to help and even finds it threatening if he has no way to control it.

The bell is obviously a case in point. It is his toy gun.

Instead of using behavior which will lead to constructive results, Boris constantly injects horseback TA, which does not. Constructive results come from risk based on awareness. TA can be useful to bring one to the point of that awareness and so make an informed decision. But the analysis itself does not produce change. Indeed, it may even be used as an excuse for avoiding it! (Fig. 15.3)

Boris appears to have a scared Child and to be using his Parent to protect it. So his Parent, by faulting Stanley's behavior, defends his threatened Child. There is no rational justification for this fear, but it is there, messing up Boris's perception of the situation. Controlling Parent behavior is his way of dealing with it. The unknown, no matter how benign it is, never penetrates his wall of games. His gamey way of avoiding reality is to keep shifting into analysis at a superficial level, before it's possible to deal with any real issues.

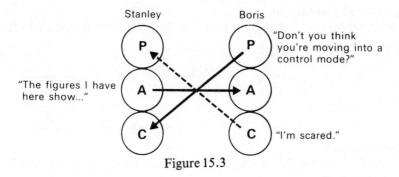

Figure 15.3

He keeps firing away throughout the meeting and so it ends with no communication, no problems solved and not even any coffee served. All the participants will have saved enough brown stamps to cash them in on Boris at the next meeting. The prize could be to play a huge game of *NIGYSOB* with him for endorsing TA! It's horrible to imagine. It would make Boris (and me) wish he had never opened the Pandora's Box of TA.

What would you do to head off this impending disaster? Could Boris's Adult tolerate some TA behavior that may be sloppy but ends in results, rather than insisting on universal TA precision tht ends in games? The thing to keep in mind for Boris (and me and you) is that TA is not a weapon to be used by our Parent; it is a tool to be applied by our Adult to free up our gutsy, wonderful, creative Child. The moral to this story is that TA should be used with discretion on others and with suitable objectivity and candor on oneself.

---

## Awareness Format

Revise the script by writing your own version of this dialogue, which has ended so badly. Use the Awareness Format to do it, and then compare your version with ours. A sample for the Awareness Format is provided in the appendix.

### I. Tapes
Change Boris's Child tape ("I get scared when things get out of control.") into an Adult statement.

Adult: _____

_____

Change Boris's Parent tape ("Always be gracious.") into an Adult statement.

Adult: _____

_____

## II. Key Crossed Transaction
Change the crossed transaction (see Fig. 15.1) to make it complementary.

Boris: _____

_____

Stanley: _____

_____

## III. Ulterior Message
Change Boris's Ulterior Message ("We're watching for your slipups.") into an Adult statement.

Adult: _____

_____

## IV. Role
Change what Boris said in his Persecutor role to an Adult statement.
Persecutor: "I'm going to ring this little bell..."

Adult: _____

_____

## V. Style
On a scale from 1 to 10 grade the applicability of each criterion from Boris's point of view. (See the introduction to this book for a detailed explanation of the criteria.)

Grade
1 to 10

A. A Developmental style may be effective:

  1. The Adult is available in the other person.      _____

  2. A joint decision is important.      _____

  3. An impasse has been reached and a new approach is desired.      _____

  4. There is time for study and discussion.      _____

B. A Controlling style may be effective:

  1. The chief priority is to get the task done as soon as possible.      _____

  2. You intend to direct the project in your own way.      _____

  3. Ready assent is forthcoming from the other person's Child.      _____

  4. Negotiation is futile, and you control all the alternatives.      _____

C. A Relinquishing style may be effective:

  1. The other person has relevant information which you do not possess.      _____

   2. The other person's Child is upset and needs your Nurturing Parent. _____

   3. Development of the other person's autonomy is the most important objective. _____

   4. The other person is autonomous, yet a caring relationship still exists. _____

D. A Defensive style may be effective:

   1. Your Child is confused or frustrated. _____

   2. Participation is against the moral standards of your Parent. _____

   3. Your support is not required. _____

   4. You are aware that games are being played. _____

Fill in the criteria score chart below according to the numbers indicated for each style. Use the criteria score chart to select a transactional style which is designed to effectively achieve Boris's Desired Result.

### Criteria Score Chart

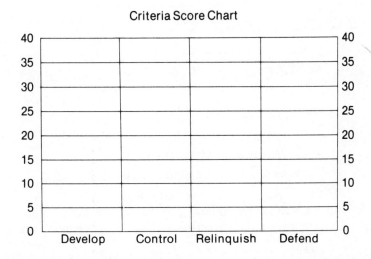

If another style is graded close to the highest one on your chart, you may want to incorporate that in your approach. Both may be appropriate at different times in the dialogue or discussion.

### *Strategy*

1. What style is indicated for the Improved Dialogue? _____

_____

2. Make some notes on how Boris's strategy might be improved, using the style indicated.

_____

_____

_____

_____

_____

_____

_____

_____

_____

_____

_____

_____

Now read the Improved Dialogue and compare it with what you have written in Sections I through V.

## THE IMPROVED DIALOGUE
### Problem Solving by Committee Meeting

In our introduction to this book, we pointed out that you would see interplay between the collaborators and that it might be interesting to look for the crossed transactions _within the book_. . . and to discern the Parent-Adult-Child tapes being played within the chapters.

This last chapter has a multiple purpose. Of course, there are aspects of it that lend themselves quite legitimately to Transactional Analysis. The fact is, however, that your playwright has allowed his Child to get loose (helped along by a good deal of Adult-based information) and handed our analyst what amounts to a well-nigh impossible situation. In addition, we have illustrated with impact the possible _misuse_ of TA training.

First, a quick look at the interplay between collaborators. Writing this book has, of course, involved a training experience in TA for this playwright. Since we've been learning together, is it possible you've drawn a diagram of one of the things that happened between the analyst and the playwright? Here's what it might look like:

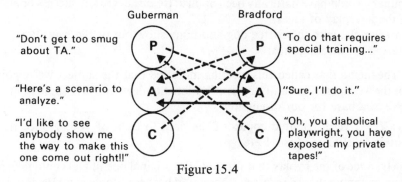

Guberman

Bradford

"Don't get too smug about TA."

"To do that requires special training..."

"Here's a scenario to analyze."

"Sure, I'll do it."

"I'd like to see anybody show me the way to make this one come out right!!"

"Oh, you diabolical playwright, you have exposed my private tapes!"

Figure 15.4

We've had an interplay between Child personalities, but, as can frequently happen, this interplay has had some value. It stimulated very Adult conclusions and (probably most important) it made the scenario and the discussion of it amusing. *We have, we believe, hooked your childish desire to be amused to get a powerful message over to your adult consciousness.*

That message is multifaceted. Transactional Analysis is not a simplistic game that solves problems with catch-phrases. If TA is to be the dominant topic of a discussion it cannot share idea-space with other subjects and there is nothing wrong with involving all facets of the personality (Adult, Parent, Child) in the transaction if the *final result* is the meshing of Adult-oriented concepts.

There is no way to write an Improved Transaction per se for this chapter. It would be unfair to our readers and an exercise in fictional playwrighting for the authors. Clearly, Boris is not by any means a mirror of the personality of any one person—much less my co-author! I'm not certain what memory tapes my playlet set in motion within my TA analyst colleague, but Boris is unique. He enjoys most of the worst attributes of the not-quite-ready-for-prime-time executive who has been exposed to a little psychological insight.

Unfortunately, there *are* Borises in the business and the social world. And there *are* meetings wherein one concept or another, reduced to the level of a fad, go berserk.

There are several points within the scenario at which Boris could save the day. We will look at some of them in a segmented manner. However, it is important to recognize that our protagonist displays certain weaknesses as an executive that strain the imagination. First, Boris clearly didn't understand what he heard about TA or he would never have shown up with the bell. Also, on a simple organizational or administrative basis, the coffee fiasco had no reason to exist; a well-organized executive who felt that refreshments should be present at such a meeting would have arranged for a selection to be available beforehand. Further, on an administrative level, Boris should have had at least a general idea of what the participants would be able to contribute to the problem solving.

Given the administrative competence that should exist in a person holding a position of the importance of Boris's, some of the principles discussed in the recent TA seminars would have naturally been applied (to one degree of success or another) during the interplay of ideas.

For example, with the coffee dog-and-pony show out of the way, Boris would have started the meeting thus:

**Boris:** The memo that called this meeting indicated that the subject we're going to tackle is the weaknesses in SaniBaby distribution. Stanley, you have some figures that can serve as a base for our discussion.

**Stanley:** Yes. I've distributed copies of the data to each of you. Notice that the distribution level in food is... etc.

Obviously, none of the byplay that followed the original opening(s) could take place. However, assuming that the crossed transaction between Stanley and Peter did occur as the meeting went on...

**Peter:** Yes, I see we're much weaker in drug than in food...

**Stanley:** It's not quite that simple. It may look that way, but in point of fact it's the other way around.

**Peter:** But 63% is a good bit higher than 43%, right?

**Maria:** Peter, why don't you shut up and let Stanley finish.

**Boris:** Peter has a valid question, of course. But I'm sure that Stanley hasn't simply tried to confuse the issue... Stan, what is the basis for your conclusion?

Here, Boris has addressed the problem rather than launching into a TA diatribe. He has, additionally, exercised some Parent-based control that any meeting sorely needs from time to time. The violent clash that takes place later in the scene as Peter allows his Child to shriek has been forestalled.

Note that the waiting-for-coffee motif is also used as a crutch in this scenario. When Maria is fed up with the course of the meeting, instead of making a constructive effort to salvage it she moans "I could sure use that coffee right about now..." With the crutch gone, she might, even at that far-gone state of this disastrous meeting, have made a constructive statement like, "Look, I think the conclusions that our agency reached might provide some light on the subject. May I summarize our report?" Who knows—she might even have brought the confused Boris out of his TA Wonderland.

## Awareness Format Applied to Your Own Situation

### I. Background
Describe briefly a situation in which you have had a responsible part and are not satisfied with the results:

_____

_____

_____

### II. Desired Result
What was your Desired Result? _____

_____

### III. Key Crossed Transaction
In that situation identify a key crossed transaction in which the response came from the Parent or the Child in the other person.

What you said: _____

_____

The response: _____

_____

Diagram your crossed transaction:

P    P

A    A

C    C

### IV. Tapes
Imagine yourself as you were when you were a very young child and think of an experience which is similar to the one you have just described. Be aware of the people who appear in your mind's eye, what you felt and what you were trying to say to them.

In the recent situation which you have just described, what appears to be the Child tape influencing your behavior from that old scene in your past?

Child tape: _____

_____

Change your Child tape into an Adult statement:

Adult: _____

_____

What appears to be your Parent tape? If you need to, go back to the memory you just retrieved for an awareness of that tape.

Parent tape: _____

_____

Change your Parent tape into an Adult statement:

Adult: _____

_____

## V. Ulterior Message

What Ulterior Message did you send to the other person? You can spot your Ulterior Message by examining your Parent and Child tapes to see how they exerted a negative influence on your transactional style in that situation.

Your Ulterior Message: _____

_____

## VI. Basic Life Position

Check out your feelings in that situation. What Basic Life Position do they seem to indicate?

Check one:  ☐ I'm not-OK—you're OK.
            ☐ I'm not-OK—you're not-OK.
            ☐ I'm OK—you're not-OK.
            ☐ I'm OK—you're OK.

What is the feeling? _____

## VII. Game Awareness

Now you can see how the parts of your game fall into place. Write here your Desired Result (see II above).

_____

Write here your Ulterior Message (see V above).

_____

Write here the response you got in the crossed transaction (see III above).

_____

Write here your Basic Life Position in that situation (see VI above) and the feeling that goes with it.

Basic Life Position:_____

Feeling: _____

What game seems to be indicated here?

Name: _____

To get out of that game, change your Ulterior Message in that game into an Adult statement.

Adult: _____

_____

## VIII. Role

What role were you playing in that game? Check one:

☐ Persecutor    ☐ Victim    ☐ Rescuer

Describe what you said or did to play that role.

_____

_____

Change that to an Adult behavior or statement:

Adult: _____

_____

## IX. Style

On a scale from 1 to 10 grade the applicability of each criterion from your point of view. (See the introduction to this book for a detailed explanation of the criteria.)

Grade
1 to 10

A. A Developmental style may be effective:

1. The Adult is available in the other person.          _____

2. A joint decision is important.                       _____

3. An impasse has been reached and a new approach is desired.   _____

4. There is time for study and discussion.              _____

B. A Controlling style may be effective:

1. The chief priority is to get the task done as soon as possible. _____

2. You intend to direct the project in your own way. _____

3. Ready assent is forthcoming from the other person's Child. _____

4. Negotiation is futile, and you control all the alternatives. _____

C. A Relinquishing style may be effective:

1. The other person has relevant information which you do not possess. _____

2. The other person's Child is upset and needs your Nurturing Parent. _____

3. Development of the other person's autonomy is the most important objective. _____

4. The other person is autonomous, yet a caring relationship still exists. _____

D. A Defensive style may be effective:

1. Your Child is confused or frustrated. _____

2. Participation is against the moral standards of your Parent. _____

3. Your support is not required. _____

4. You are aware that games are being played. _____

Fill in the criteria score chart below, Use the criteria score chart to develop a transactional strategy that will effectively attain your Desired Result.

Criteria Score Chart

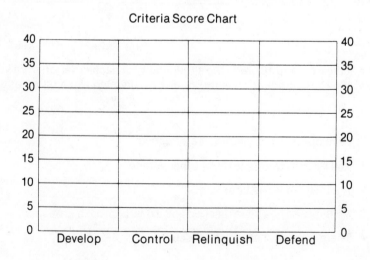

If some other style appears to be close to another one on your chart, you may want to incorporate that in your approach. Both may be appropriate at different times in the dialogue or discussion.

### *Strategy*

1. What style is indicated for your Improved Dialogue?

_____

2. Look over carefully what you have written in Sections I-IX and use it to help yourself decide how to implement that style. Then make some notes on what you will do:

_____
_____
_____
_____
_____
_____
_____
_____
_____
_____

3. When will you do it? _____

_____

# Glossary

**Adult ego state.** The part of the personality which organizes information on the basis of here-and-now observation. It operates dispassionately and without moral judgment.

**Apparent message.** What appears to be going on in a situation at a superficial level.

**Autonomous.** Taking responsibility for oneself—including one's feelings and one's condition in life. Autonomous people do not let their lives be controlled by old tapes, but run the show themselves through their awareness in the here and now.

**Awareness.** Consciousness at the Adult level of the interpersonal dynamics involved in a situation.

**Awareness Format.** A questionnaire that allows one to systematically determine the best options for communication in a given situation.

**Bad feeling.** The feeling state at the final conclusion of a game. Note that there are authentic bad feelings which are nongamey. These come from the tragedies of life. Gamey bad feelings are phoney, recurrent and unnecessary, though they seem real at the time.

**Basic Life Position.** An attitude based on feeling, not fact, about one's self and others, established early in life.

**Child ego state.** The part of the personality that responds in a direct emotional way to any situation. Early life experiences may condition the Child so that its responses are less natural or spontaneous than they might be. But those limitations can be changed later through awareness and redecision.

**Child tapes.** Feelings experienced early in life which are recorded and stored in the brain. In later years, they may seem real enough to influence attitudes and behavior.

**Complementary transaction.** A transaction in which the response fits neatly with the stimulus. Occurs, for example, when a Parent-to-Child stimulus is met by a Child-to-Parent response.

**Controlling style.** A style of communication which directs other people by telling them what to do and how to do it.

**Critical Parent.** That aspect of the Parent ego state which is extremely negative toward one's self and others.

**Crossed transaction.** An impasse in communication, which occurs when two people are talking past each other and are out of contact. Occurs, for example, when an Adult-to-Adult stimulus is met by a Parent-to-Child response.

**Defensive style.** A communication style which does not get involved in a situation and in which strokes are withheld.

**Desired Result.** The conscious objective chosen to be attained in a situation.

**Developmental style.** A style of communication in which there is an exchange of ideas which leads to problem solving.

**Drama triangle.** A simple diagram indicating how the Persecutor, Rescuer and Victim roles interact.

**Ego state.** One of the three states of mind—Parent, Adult or Child—that controls a response to a situation.

**Game.** A negative form of behavior ending dramatically but without constructive results. Berne's definition: "A series of ongoing complementary ulterior transactions ending in a well defined, predictable payoff."

**Hidden message.** An ulterior message, conveyed through nonverbal behavior or implied verbally.

**Intimacy.** A way to structure time and stroking that is characterized by candor, openness and trust.

**Not-OK Child.** A feeling of inadequacy about one's self (old tapes left over from childhood) which may interfere with here-and-now transactions.

**Nurturing Parent.** That aspect of the Parent ego state which is concerned for the welfare of one's self and others.

**Parent ego state.** The part of the personality that responds to situations in the same way as one's parents did. It is oriented toward the past rather than the here and now.

**Parent tapes.** Impressions of parents and other authority figures stored in the brain, which control or influence behavior.

**Permission.** Approval from the Parent ego state for a certain kind of Child behavior or feeling.

**Persecutor.** A person who viciously attacks others without seriously considering any positive qualities they might have.

**Relinquishing style.** A communication style which lets the other person take the initiative, but follows it closely.

**Rescuer.** A person who only "tries" to help and is threatened by the autonomy of the one who relies on him or her for aid.

**Role.** A part played in a script.

**Role switch.** The shift from one role to another, such as from Victim to Persecutor, which occurs when sufficient stamps are collected to qualify for that prize.

**Script.** A program for the way one's life will go, based on a set of decisions made early in the life experience about one's self and others which gives it coherency. Scripting may limit autonomy later in life.

**Script theme.** A phrase which captures the essence of a script, like a newspaper headline.

**Spontaneity.** Freedom to respond, uncontrolled by old tapes, in a given situation.

**Stamp collecting.** The practice of seeking out experiences that will evoke some favored mode of feeling (good or bad), each experience being the equivalent of a "stamp" to save and cash in at the right moment. Gold stamps are good feelings saved up for a prize such as a holiday to which one feels entitled. Brown stamps are bad feelings saved up for a prize such as going on a binge, for which one feels justified. The more stamps collected, the greater the prize, just as with the trading stamps issued by supermarkets.

**Stroke.** The basic unit of social interaction, by which one person signals recognition of another.

**Time structuring.** The six ways in which strokes are exchanged, i.e., withdrawal, rituals, pastimes, activities, games and intimacy.

**Transaction.** An exchange of strokes.

**Transactional Analysis.** A system for understanding human behavior devised by Eric Berne, consisting of Structural Analysis, Transactional Analysis, Game Analysis, and Script Analysis.

**Transactional Awareness.** A system for checking out the best options for communication and developing an effective strategy. This is based on Transactional Analysis. Transactional Awareness is a registered trademark of Transactional Awareness, Inc.

**Ulterior message.** A hidden meaning communicated without awareness.

**Ulterior transaction.** An exchange in which both parties outwardly operate from certain ego states but in fact have exchanged messages from a different set of ego states.

**Victim.** A person who unrealistically believes that others are attacking him and that he cannot protect himself.

# Appendix

## Appendix: Sample Awareness Format

### I. Tapes

In changing Sam's tape to an Adult statement, you are substituting for an unconscious influence—the tape—an awareness of what behavior is called for in the here-and-now transaction.

If you imagine yourself as that character in the dialogue, being influenced by this tape, you can imagine how to respond after his Adult has checked it out. Put that response into words and you have the Adult statement.

Your answer may differ from the example shown.

Change Sam's Child tape ("I'm scared your standards are too high.") into an Adult statement.

Adult: *I know this is a challenge. Let me think about ways to meet it effectively.*

Change Sam's Parent tape ("Make a good impression, Son.") into an Adult statement.

Adult: *I will listen carefully first and then respond.*

### II. Key Crossed Transaction

If Sam used a different—more Adult—stimulus, he would get a different response.

Here is an example of how we made it come out differently and uncrossed the transaction. Try putting it in your own words.

Change the crossed transaction (see Fig. 1.1) to make it complementary.

Sam: *I'm pretty sure you'll find the background information fairly complete, Mr. Dubious, but I'll be glad to fill in any blanks.*

Harry: *Yes, well, I will have a few questions.*

### III. Ulterior Message

Sam is not aware of his Ulterior Message. But if he were, what message would he deliver instead?

See our example and try one of your own.

Change Sam's Ulterior Message ("Tell me I don't qualify.") into an Adult statement.

Adult: *I came here prepared to accept your offer.*

## IV. Role

Sam is not aware of his Victim role. If he were, what would he say instead? See our example and then try working on an improved response yourself.

Change what Sam said in his Victim role to an Adult statement.
Victim: "They went bankrupt, which is why I'm available."

Adult: *I wasn't in on the capital investment setup and I wasn't consulted or informed about the real estate situation. I can say this — my store showed an operating profit each year.*

## V. Style

Here is a sample of how the criteria might be graded and the score chart filled out. We used the score chart to make some notes on how Sam's style might be improved. Try it yourself.

What the criteria indicate is more than just what the numbers add up to. One criterion may outweigh others because it is particularly significant.

There is an explanation of each criterion in the introduction to this book.

|  | Grade 1 to 10 |
|---|---|
| A. A Developmental style may be effective: | |
| 1. The Adult is available in the other person. | 5 |
| 2. A joint decision is important. | 5 |
| 3. An impasse has been reached and a new approach is desired. | 5 |
| 4. There is time for study and discussion. | |
| B. A Controlling style may be effective: | |
| 1. The chief priority is to get the task done as soon as possible. | |
| 2. You intend to direct the project in your own way. | |
| 3. Ready assent is forthcoming from the other person's Child. | |
| 4. Negotiation is futile, and you control all the alternatives. | |

C. A Relinquishing style may be effective:

1. The other person has relevant information which you do not possess. ___10___

2. The other person's Child is upset and needs your Nurturing Parent. _____

3. Development of the other person's autonomy is the most important objective. _____

4. The other person is autonomous, yet a caring relationship still exists. _____

D. A Defensive style may be effective:

1. Your Child is confused or frustrated. _____

2. Participation is against the moral standards of your Parent. _____

3. Your support is not required. _____

4. You are aware that games are being played. _____

Fill in the criteria score chart below according to the numbers indicated for each style. Use the criteria score chart to select a transactional style which is designed to effectively achieve Sam's Desired Result.

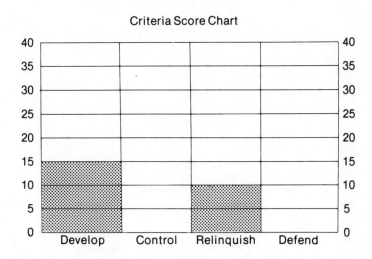

Criteria Score Chart

If another style is graded close to the highest one on your chart, you may want to incorporate that in your approach. Both may be appropriate at different times in the dialogue or discussion.

*Strategy*

1. What style is indicated for the Improved Dialogue?   Develop-
Relinquish

2. Make some notes on how Sam's strategy might be improved, using the style indicated.

As the criteria indicate, Sam has to develop a style that shifts between Developing and Relinquishing. He must listen carefully and then confidently give the specific information required. Also, he needs to present himself as a person who can take responsibility and make decisions effectively.